The Military Intervenes

WITHDRAWN

The Military Intervenes

CASE STUDIES IN

POLITICAL DEVELOPMENT

EDITED BY HENRY BIENEN
Assistant Professor of Politics, Princeton University, and Faculty Associate, Center of International Studies

RUSSELL SAGE FOUNDATION

NEW YORK 1968

PUBLICATIONS OF RUSSELL SAGE FOUNDATION

Russell Sage Foundation was established in 1907 by Mrs. Russell Sage for the improvement of social and living conditions in the United States. In carrying out its purpose the Foundation conducts research under the direction of members of the staff or in close collaboration with other institutions, and supports programs designed to improve the utilization of social science knowledge. As an integral part of its operations, the Foundation from time to time publishes books or pamphlets resulting from these activities. Publication under the imprint of the Foundation does not necessarily imply agreement by the Foundation, its Trustees, or its staff with the interpretations or conclusions of the authors.

Library of Congress Catalog Card Number: 67-31395

PRINTED IN THE UNITED STATES OF AMERICA BY
CONNECTICUT PRINTERS, INC., HARTFORD, CONNECTICUT

The Contributors

HENRY BIENEN
> *Department of Politics, Center of International Studies,*
> *Princeton University*

DONALD N. LEVINE
> *Department of Sociology, University of Chicago*

JAE SOUK SOHN
> *Department of Political Science, Seoul National University*

PHILIP B. SPRINGER
> *Sociologist, Office of United States Secretary of Labor*

NUR YALMAN
> *Department of Anthropology, University of Chicago*

ARISTIDE R. ZOLBERG
> *Department of Political Science, University of Chicago*

Contents

Preface

RESEARCH and analysis on the political role of the military in the developing nations has of necessity been general and concerned with formulating hypotheses and "model building." In many parts of the world, military government is very new and detailed descriptions of its operations are difficult to construct. The major emphasis in the work to date has been on describing the political context which precipitates military intervention in domestic politics. In addition, an important theme has been the analysis of the military as a social institution in order to determine its potentialities and limitations for supplying political leadership.

The research essays in *The Military Intervenes* represent a significant next step. The standpoint is that of the case study in varying degrees of depth. The central problematic issue shifts from the conditions under which the military intervenes to a concern with the mechanisms of intervention and the consequences of such intervention. Existing viewpoints divide those authors who assign broad and extensive potentialities for the military in "political development" from those who point to pervasive limitations of the military to create political institutions appropriate for sustained economic growth and social development. Henry Bienen, the editor of this volume, concludes that the materials he has assembled supply evidence which highlights the powerful constraints that operate to narrow the role of the military per se as effective agents of political change.

These case studies do not offer a representative sample and there are real questions as to the meaning of representativeness for such a universe of events. In part, these studies are the result of the contributors' interests and opportunities for undertaking field research. In each case, the author has had direct and prolonged contact with the area and institutions about which he writes. But the results do present a wide range of the political circumstances and institutional settings that operate when the military seeks to exercise political power.

First, it is of historical note to point out that a personal autocracy in a traditional regime is able temporarily to repress the revolutionary activities of a new and young generation of officer cadres (Ethiopia). The number of countries with this type of government is limited and their vulnerability to political revolution increases as they haltingly seek to modernize. Second, it is of great significance to analyze those attempted military take-overs which have failed because they are more like mutinies than armed interventions (Kenya, Uganda, and Tanganyika). These are conditions under which the armed forces are poorly organized and have limited resources, and their demands are, in effect, for improved "conditions of employment." Even such mutinies supply a school for political education for military forces untried in politics.

Third, it is of central importance to explore those cases where the military has been in power for a long period of time. In Latin America, military regimes have ruled long enough to observe the political liabilities that accrue to them even where an outright take-over follows widespread ineffectiveness and repression. One pattern of rule by military oligarchy is an institutionalized coup and counter-coup among officer factions as a method of regulating political demands (Argentina). Such a pattern is highly unstable and not productive of economic and social development. However, the range of military patterns of intervention includes the emergence of a strong sense of self-restraint which leads the military to accept a role of umpire among competing political groups (Turkey). A sense of realism can also lead the military to create a mass party with the full symbolic equipment and organization of a civilian party (South Korea).

These case studies set the stage for a continuing strategy of analyzing "successful" and "unsuccessful" military interventions. They help to give meaning to the hypothesis that the process of military intervention is not irreversible, but if political change must wait for the breakdown of a military oligarchy, its outcome will not be conducive to an orderly and humane process of modernization. Thus, the "Ataturk" model emerges both as a political goal and a bench mark for comparative analysis. What are the institutional and political conditions under which the military takes active steps to disengage itself from political involvements versus the alternative conditions under which it merely seeks to "exercise" power? The clarity and direction of United States foreign and military assistance policy is certainly one of the relevant variables.

These essays are an outgrowth of the work of the Inter-University Seminar on Armed Forces and Society, which is supported by Russell Sage Foundation. The Inter-University Seminar seeks to bring together university sociologists and political scientists concerned with the impact of military institutions on society both in the United States and throughout the world. We wish to express our profound gratitude to Russell Sage Foundation, and especially to Orville G. Brim, Jr., and Leonard S. Cottrell, Jr., for their creative leadership which has made this experiment in collaborative research possible. Sponsorship by Russell Sage Foundation, with its long tradition of independent scholarship, has given us an effective basis for work on the international level during a period in which the study of armed forces and society on a cross-national basis is by no means an uncomplicated or simple task. The authors have sought to maintain a detached and objective point of view while proceeding in a responsible fashion.

The Inter-University Seminar has been increasingly able to cooperate with foreign scholars, since it is clear that a multilateral approach contributes to effective scholarship and avoids the overtones of intellectual imperialism. As a result, its members were actively involved in the working group on "Militarism and the Professional Military Man" of the International Sociological Association's Sixth World Congress in Evian, France, in September, 1966. At the Evian conference, social scientists from the United States, Western and Eastern Europe, the USSR, South America, and the Far East convened to examine research problems involving the study of armed forces and society. The research papers of this conference have been prepared for publication by Jacques van Doorn, Netherlands Economic Institute, under the title *Armed Forces and Society: Sociological Essays* (Mouton and Company, The Hague, 1968).

As an outgrowth of the Evian meetings, a conference was held in London in September, 1967, with wider representation from the Far East, Africa, and South America, that focused on the military and social change. These papers will constitute a second volume in the series edited by van Doorn, under the title *The Military Profession and Military Regimes,* also to be published in 1968 by Mouton and Company.

The Inter-University Seminar has an ongoing program of individual research and intellectual discussion within a cross-national perspective.

In my opinion, the efforts of Henry Bienen and his associates are representative of the new generation of research scholars who have the boldness of character and the analytical skills to probe fundamental issues in comparative research which previous generations avoided or only contemplated at a distance.

MORRIS JANOWITZ
Chairman, Inter-University Seminar
on Armed Forces and Society

University of Chicago
October, 1967

Introduction

A NUMBER of studies of developing countries have pointed out that in these areas the military is the best organized institution and therefore is in the best position "to give expression to the national will."[1] This kind of analysis considers discipline and organization to be the key qualities necessary for institutions to act with political effect. Similarly, because the military is the strongest force in society (that is, it can intervene successfully against other groups), it has been thought that only a military regime can have the power to prevail against communist parties.[2] More positively, military elites have been claimed to be dynamic forces for modernization. The military thus is thought to be not only a force which can oppose the quasi-militarily organized communist parties, but also one which can bring order out of disorder in developing countries. The military is considered an instrument of change, a nation-builder, or a melting pot in which various heterogeneous elements are unified as the military imposes its own sense of discipline and its own rational norms.[3]

No doubt many American government officials, military leaders, and academicians believe that the military in the developing areas is the best counterforce against both internal and external disruption. Some rather pessimistic observers believe that at least the armed forces provide something of a guarantee against the sort of chaos which would ultimately make development, hard as it is now, almost impossible.[4] Others have higher hopes for the military regimes, believing that they can and will be more effective than political parties in modernizing their societies.[5] An accurate appraisal of the role of the military in fostering political development is of vital importance not only for the study of the countries themselves but also as the basis for an evaluation of American military assistance programs to these areas.[6]

The case studies in this volume present analyses of specific military interventions in order to test some propositions presented in more general treatments of the subject.[7] At the same time, a common theme runs through all the case studies—the limits of the military in fostering modernization. The studies clearly show the obstacles to modernization, political stability, and public order that are created during the process of intervention or take-over. They support the proposition that it is easier for the military to accumulate power than to govern as a ruling group.[8] This point, however, has been made with varying degrees of emphasis and clarity by all the observers we have cited.[9] We try to examine why it is true by exploring the interventions themselves. We come to grips with the subject of "armed forces and society" by elaborating the specific structure, composition, and resources of the military forces, the political context of involvement in a crisis, and the social environment in which the military acts. We describe the factors which incline the military toward intervention and which limit its political capacity.

MILITARY INTERVENTIONS

THE very terms "new nations" and "underdeveloped" or "developing areas" reflect our shared assumption that similar political, economic, and social problems and goals characterize a host of states in Asia, Africa, and Latin America. These are societies with low levels of economic productivity and high degrees of social cleavage. They can be described in terms of political gaps between rulers and ruled, economic gaps between classes, and social and cultural gaps between linguistic, racial, or ethnic groups.[10] Thus the polities of these societies are fragile, unstable, and porous. As tensions rise, the military appears to be an effective source of stability when other elites have lost legitimacy because they have been unable to solve problems. As Shils puts it, "Military rule is one of several practicable and apparently stable alternatives when parliamentary, democratic regimes falter."[11]

Indeed, many observers of the military in developing areas have noted that take-over by the military generally follows a collapse or discrediting of democratic-type institutions. As Aristide R. Zolberg points out in his study, "Military Intervention in the New States of Tropical Africa: Elements of Comparative Analysis," it appeared for a time that the one-party states of West Africa were immune from military take-overs. And in general, it was believed that strong one-party or mass-party authoritarian regimes would not be so easily displaced by military intervention.[12] This line of analysis was correct insofar as it pointed to the effectiveness of strong party organizations in warding off coups and the legitimacy of ruling parties in obviating them. The point is: Where, excluding Asian communist parties, are the strong ruling mass parties in the underdeveloped countries?[13]

The Ghanaian military removed Nkrumah and the Convention People's Party with no more ostensible difficulty than the armed forces faced in essentially party-less systems elsewhere in Africa. This particular civilian elite could not depend on the personal authority of the leader or the prestige of the party which brought the country to independence to forestall a military take-over. Where political parties are effective in developmental tasks, and where leaders remain personally popular, civilian elites may ride out a troubled period, provided the military is not highly motivated to intervene for its own interests. But it is becoming clear that the "mass" parties of Africa have little more organizational strength and cohesion than discredited parties in Asia and Latin America. Nor do the remaining ruling African single parties appear to have enough grass-roots support which could be translated into political strength to survive a storm which might arise from the discontent of some group or from a deteriorating economic situation.

The case studies show that a unified military can take power with relative ease in Asia, Africa, and Latin America. The military is thus a "heavy institution" in underdeveloped countries[14] and can act with authority because it is first and foremost an institution of force with organizational features that give it the capacity to be effective in intervening against a civilian regime.[15] Furthermore, the military is often, but not always, the most modern institution in terms of its advanced technology, educated elite, absorption of rational norms, division of labor, and exposure to western influence.[16] Although these factors do not necessarily make the military a guarantor of stability, they do facilitate decisive action in a crisis.

Recent events in Africa show that military usurpation can be a threat even when the military does not meet the requirements of full-fledged armed forces. An army with a small indigenous officer corps, limited mobility and firepower, and a very small total force compared to the population may not meet the minimum formal requirements of what we usually call a military force. Nonetheless, such a force can seize power where few organized groups participate in the political process.

Civilian rule ends, by definition, when the armed forces take over. But there are obvious differences in the nature of termination of civilian rule. The army may move in a crisis with great reluctance but with unity, as Nur Yalman argues in his case study, "Intervention and Extrication: The Officer Corps in the Turkish Crisis." Or an element of the army may seize on a political crisis to gain power and status for itself within society and within a divided military, as Jae Souk Sohn describes the case in Korea in his study, "Political Dominance and Political Failure: The Role of the Military in the Republic of Korea." The military may act as an interest group and may not be motivated by any particular crisis, as shown in my study, "Public Order and the Military in Africa: Mutinies in Kenya, Uganda, and Tanganyika." In such a situation, the military may create rather than react to a crisis.

Unity within the army may be a double-edged sword. Cohesion allows the army to move successfully, as in Turkey; lack of it may lead to failure, as Donald Levine shows was the case in Ethiopia. In his study, "The Military in Ethiopian Politics: Capabilities and Constraints," he argues that the Imperial Bodyguard revolt in 1960 failed because the Guards did not carry the Army with them. Similarly, Yalman shows that the second Turkish officer coup of 1962 failed because it was carried out by a minority within the officer corps. However, lack of cohesion may also promote initial coups (Korea, East Africa) and often leads to new attempts by officers to oust the original junta, as shown in Philip B. Springer's study, "Disunity and Disorder: Factional Politics in the Argentine Military."

Springer and Yalman also argue that the military intervention itself begins to split the military, if it is not already faction-ridden. This tendency is especially crucial where the military is trying to stabilize the politics of its country while maintaining a commanding position for itself. Sohn presents persuasive evidence for Korea that the more the military takes on political roles, the more vulnerable it is to loss of internal cohesion. Competition intensifies within the military across ranks, generations, and branches of the armed forces.

Our evidence shows that even though small armies can intervene easily in crises, we cannot take it for granted that they will always be able to restore order. Sometimes they may promote disorder or fall prey to it, reflecting society's disorder in their own ranks.[17] Both Zolberg's case study and mine show that the military can itself be a force for instability, as it was in the Congo, the three East African countries, Togo, and Nigeria. We might expect this tendency where military involvement in the politics of rule is just beginning, as in Sub-Saharan Africa, since the pattern of postcolonial rule is being disrupted for the first time. It is also clear from Springer's study that where military intervention becomes part of the system, the military does not always restore order; it may disrupt stability.

To rule, the army must form alliances with civilian groups. In the process, the military more and more reflects political and social divisions within society.[18] It loses legitimacy as its claim to stand above conflicting groups is called in question. No longer can the military be convincing in its assertion that it embodies the essence of nationhood, for it appears to act simply as another claimant for power beset by its own internal divisions. Furthermore, we cannot take it for granted that armed forces are indeed perceived by their populations as the carriers of nationhood. The prestige of an army may not be transferable into legitimacy for rule. It is not simply that the army is ineffective as a ruler; the indigenous political cultures of traditional or modern sectors of a country may militate against army legitimacy. In this regard, the type of takeover which transforms the army into a military oligarchy is crucial.[19] Whether the army acts in a premeditated way or reacts to a breakdown of civilian rule affects its legitimacy as ruler. And whether an army coup calls into question the rule of a particular leader, a government, or the legitimacy of a state system determines in part the new pattern which will emerge.[20]

Not all failures of civilian regimes are alike. The failure of Nkrumah, the Nigerian politicians, Olympio in Togo, Lumumba or Kasavubu in the Congo were all quite different with regard to breakdown of public order and the extent of economic dislocation. The similarity, as Zolberg explains, is in shared and durable characteristics of political life—institutional weakness, stalemate in the pursuit of modernization, and a concomitant increase in the "market value" of the military as the need for force grows. These factors are prevalent in Africa as well as in other developing areas. It now appears highly probable that extensive areas will be under military rule in Africa, and it is becoming more important to assess correctly the prospects for successful rule by the military.

AMERICAN MILITARY ASSISTANCE

THE military forces of developing nations depend on the great powers for their maintenance and growth. They are, in large measure, the creation of the United States, Great Britain, France, and the Soviet Union. Other countries sell sophisticated weapons in Asia, Africa, and Latin America. Even some countries which themselves fall within the category of developing nations resell arms they have received, produce small conventional arms, or have modest military training missions abroad, for example, the United Arab Republic. However, only the great powers can as yet supply developing nations with warships, tanks, missiles, and jet aircraft on a large scale. Moreover, because the purchase of military equipment imposes such heavy burdens on the economies of states, many of which can hardly be said to be developing, military aid is essential for them.[21]

Although the United States has not been the largest supplier of jet aircraft, tanks, warships, and missiles (if Korea, Taiwan, Japan, South Vietnam, and South and Central America are excluded), it has, of course, been a major supplier.[22] And United States grants-in-aid to developing areas under the Military Assistance Program (MAP) was well over $1 billion in 1963. It has since fallen under $500 million in 1965.[23]

American military assistance and military sales policies have been stated in Foreign Assistance Acts and elsewhere. In accordance with American political and military objectives, the United States government sells or permits sales of arms in order to: strengthen the defense forces of the free world, preserve and extend American military influence, assist in offsetting foreign exchange costs of maintaining American military bases abroad, and standardize equipment and gain acceptance for strategic and tactical concepts through use of common hardware.[24]

Military assistance and sales have been defended on the grounds that national security is strengthened by developing strong allies or by winning political and economic influence through arms programs. Arguments have been made that military assistance can stabilize a given area through balance-of-power politics and through creating strong political units which will not be targets for aggression and subversion. The creation of strong military forces to assure the independence of a country has been seen as necessary vis-à-vis external foes or internal subversion supported by outside enemies. And the idea that the military in developing countries is the most appropriate institution for modernizing or developing the nation also is used to support military assistance.

United States policy toward the developing areas hinges on the positions taken vis-à-vis the militaries. Huntington has argued that "instead of relying on the military, American policy should be directed to the creation within modernizing countries of at least one strong non-Communist political party."[25] He maintains that military coups and military juntas may spur modernization (industrialization, urbanization, literacy, broadening of political participation, rise in per capita income, increase in mass media circulation) but that they cannot produce a stable political order. Our studies show that, in many cases at least, the military does not mobilize and does not develop nonpolitical spheres. It fails in organization- and institution-building, and it fails as well to increase economic development, political participation, and other aspects of the modernization process.

However, even if we establish that the military is the institution in a specific country most likely to bring about development, American military assistance would not necessarily be appropriate. Such assistance could be dysfunctional to the maintenance or development of the military as a nation-builder. It is conceivable that the only way a military elite could be successful in bringing about economic development and social change is by restricting its own growth and the importation of military hardware. The scope, structure, and level of an aid program are a critical influence on the material resources and human energies of the recipients, which may be channeled away from certain tasks in order to handle the incoming material and personnel. Perhaps most important, the nature of the military as an instrument for change varies with its own size and structure. If the military becomes very large compared to civilian elites, it may be taking so large a share of national income that economic development will be precluded. And it may lose political effectiveness as it acquires the machinery of force.

Of course, American policy makers must take into account factors other than modernization and political development in the developing countries. They must also consider the international alignments that will be made by military elites. One danger is that United States policy will perhaps overemphasize this particular concern to the detriment of others or that the "correct" international alignment will color American views about the prospects for military success in dealing with domestic problems. This problem has special urgency because many of the new states are on the physical periphery of communist states. Even where there is no geographical proximity to communist states, containment of communism has been an overriding and quasi-military goal.

There may be grounds on which indigenous military forces and military regimes are to be supported whatever the prospects for modernization. But policy makers must at least be clear about the costs and benefits of American assistance programs. They cannot assume that the requisites of a country's development are congruent with American short-term security interests. As our studies of Korea and Ethiopia point out, already the military may possess many of the "modern" resources available in societies. Are we going to increase disproportions through military assistance programs in the name of military security, international politics, or domestic development? At the least, we ought not to be confused about the raison d'etre of such programs and their possible benefits. Aid to specific military regimes may be justified, but we ought not spuriously to hope that development and modernization are going to be inevitable or even probable outcomes. The mistakes of American military aid programs in Latin America and Asia ought not to be repeated in Africa in this regard at least.

In these pages, then, certain views about the military as a nation-builder are questioned. Even the idea that the military stands for order —rather than for goods and services—is shown to be sometimes a myth. This is not to deny that military coups *may* be a sign of development through change, nor that some military elites may modernize their societies. We cannot and do not claim that this collection of case studies is representative. However, they are not unrepresentative as to geographical area, and more important perhaps, as to type of situation, which we have broadly defined in three categories—"The Initial Involvement," "After the Seizure of Power," and "Institutionalized Intervention." The role of case studies is to test general propositions in order to support, deny, or reformulate them. These studies cast doubt on the role of the military as a modernizing and stabilizing agent under widely different conditions of the developing countries.

Furthermore, these studies point out the need for a new sophistication concerning the military. The very term "the military" implies a monolithic and homogeneous organization. Yet we see that often military forces, despite their supposed discipline and cohesion, are themselves factionalized even before they intervene as rulers or coalition forces. In addition, aid can be exploited by one branch of the military or one faction within a branch. Not a monolithic military but a politically divided military makes alliances with civilian groups and civil services.

Without such alliances, military elites cannot even hope to extend their rule and make it operative. But as they make alliances, military elites begin to act like other political groups. Alliance with civil servants may allow for maintenance of administration and public order. Foreign investments can be attracted, and balance-of-payments problems can be alleviated with aid from the International Monetary Fund. But the problem of mass support for the regime and participation of citizens in public life is not solved. Social mobilization is not brought about ipso facto by military rule. The coup which brings the military to power usually contains the seeds of internal division within the military and prospect of some future military coup.

Our point is not that failures of military regimes are unique. The failure of modernization and political development is characteristic of many newly developing states which have civilian regimes. What we show is that the militaries are prone to failure too, and that their failures can be traced to specific consequences of military coup and rule.

If this analysis has merit, American policy on military assistance, program training for foreign Service officers, and arms control must take account of it. Above all, the connection between American military policy and economic-political policy ought to be reassessed so that we can better gauge whether both policies are working toward the same goals.

HENRY BIENEN

NOTES

1. Johnson, John J., *The Military and Society in Latin America.* Stanford University Press, Stanford, Calif., 1964, p. 143.

2. See Pauker, Guy, "Southeast Asia as a Problem Area in the Next Decade," *World Politics,* vol. 11, April, 1959, esp. pp. 339–344.

3. Pye, Lucian W., "Armies in the Process of Political Modernization," in Johnson, John J., editor, *The Role of the Military in Underdeveloped Countries.* Princeton University Press, Princeton, N.J, 1962, pp. 69–90. See also "Supplement to the President's Committee to Study United States Military Assistance Programs," vol. 2. U.S. Government Printing Office, Washington, 1959.

4. Bell, M. J. V., *Army and Nation in Sub-Saharan Africa,* Adelphi Papers No. 21. Institute for Strategic Studies, London, 1956, p. 16.

5. As W. F. Gutteridge argued for Nigeria in his "Introduction" to Wood, David, *The Armed Forces of African States,* Adelphi Papers No. 27, Institute for Strategic Studies, London, 1966, p. 2.

6. Robert Packenham, in "Political Development Doctrines in the American Foreign Aid Program," *World Politics,* vol. 18, January, 1966, p. 205, notes how few are the works which use the studies of developing areas to derive guidelines useful for foreign policy makers.

7. For the most thorough and far-reaching discussion of the common organizational features of the military in new nations, see Janowitz, Morris, *The Military in the Political Development of New Nations: An Essay in Comparative Analysis,* University of Chicago Press, Chicago, 1964.

See also Johnson, John J., editor, *The Role of the Military in Underdeveloped Countries, op. cit.* Samuel Huntington's *Changing Patterns of Military Politics* (The Free Press, New York, 1962) is a collection of essays dealing with developed as well as developing areas. Most of the contributions in both these volumes range over a whole continent or geographical area; and even where there is a study of the military in one country, the treatment is not a case study of a specific intervention but rather a survey of military-civilian relations. Samuel Finer's *The Man on Horseback* (Pall Mall Press, London, 1962) ranges widely over time and space as individual cases are cited to support general statements about military intervention.

For a critical evaluation of the literature on military intervention and coups, see Lissak, Moshe, "Selected Literature of Revolutions and Coups d'État in the Developing Nations," in Janowitz, Morris, editor, *The New Military: Changing Patterns of Organization,* Russell Sage Foundation, New York, 1964, pp. 339–362.

8. Janowitz, Morris, "Organizing Multiple Goals: War Making and Arms Control," in *The New Military, op. cit.,* p. 29.

9. Finer, Samuel, *The Man on Horseback, op. cit.,* pp. 14–22; Huntington, Samuel, *Changing Patterns of Military Politics, op. cit.,* p. 36; Janowitz, Morris, *The Military in the Political Development of New Nations, op. cit.,* pp. 29, 42, 43; Shils, Edward, "The Military in the Political Development of New States," in Johnson, John J., editor, *The Role of the Military in Underdeveloped Countries, op. cit.,* pp. 33–44; Pye, Lucian W., in Johnson, editor, *op. cit.,* p. 79.

10. For a discussion of "gaps," see Shils, Edward, in Johnson, editor, *op. cit.,* pp. 14–33.

11. *Ibid.,* p. 9.

12. *Ibid.;* also see Janowitz, Morris, *The Military in the Political Development of New Nations, op. cit.,* pp. 29, 103; Gutteridge, William, *Armed Forces in New States,* Oxford University Press, New York, 1962, p. 67.

13. We do not consider the Chinese, North Korean, or North Vietnamese pattern of civilian-military relations. So far no clear-cut military intervention to replace party control has appeared. But whether the communist parties are militarized, or whether effective civilian control exists, or even whether we should pose civilian-military distinctions in terms we use elsewhere are questions for investigation.

14. Greene, Fred, "Toward Understanding Military Coups," *African Report,* vol. 2, February, 1966, pp. 10–14.

15. Janowitz, Morris, *The Military in the Political Development of New Nations, op. cit.,* pp. 31–32.

16. Pye, Lucian W., in Johnson, editor, *op. cit.,* pp. 73–80.

17. See an editorial in *West Africa,* no. 2535, January 1, 1966, which argued that the military could easily intervene, particularly when central power was "weak, demoralized, or discredited," and could restore some degree of order, but would find governing no easy task.

18. As Samuel Huntington in *Changing Patterns of Military Politics* points out. *Op. cit.,* p. 36.

19. Janowitz, Morris, *The Military in the Political Development of New Nations, op. cit.,* p. 85.

20. *Ibid.,* pp. 16, 85, 113.

21. This aid may be on a grant-in-aid (gift) basis, or it may be arranged through terms of purchase (price, interest on loans, length of payment), which facilitate payment. Training programs either in the developing country or in the donor nation are another form of aid.

22. For statistics on United States export of arms to developing nations, see Sutton, John L., and Geoffrey Kemp, *Arms to Developing Countries,* Adelphi Papers No. 28, Institute for Strategic Studies, London, 1966.

23. *Ibid.,* p. 44, citing as a source United States Department of Defense *Military Assistance Facts,* 1965, and *Information and Guidance on Military Assistance,* 1964. The figures for 1965 are estimated by the Department of Defense.

24. *Ibid.,* citing *Information and Guidance on Military Assistance,* Directorate of Military Assistance, Headquarters, United States Air Force, 9th edition, 1965.

25. Huntington, Samuel, "Political Development and Political Decay," *World Politics,* vol. 17, April, 1965, p. 429. Huntington distinguishes between political development and modernization (p. 393). Political development is conceived as a process independent of, although affected by, the process of modernization. Political development is defined by him as the institutionalization of political organizations and procedures.

PART ONE

The Initial Involvement:
Sub-Saharan Africa

PART ONE

The Initial Involvement:
Sub-Saharan Africa

WITHIN the developing areas, Africa now provides us with the most numerous examples of the initial phase of military intervention. The military may present its demands either by using or threatening to use force; it may settle conflicts between civilian contenders; or it may itself take over government. Africa is more frequently in this beginning phase compared to Asia, the Middle East, and Latin America, because newly independent African states are the most recent arrivals on the world scene.

There are still countries elsewhere in the developing areas which have never had military coups or overt military disruptions.[1] (It is hard to determine whether the military has intervened to settle disputes as a final arbitrator because this may not always be done openly.) But many countries of Asia, Africa, and Latin America have had either long-standing military rule or repeated interventions by the military in determining governments and policies. In Africa, after a period of only a few years of independent civilian government, the military has intervened in a growing number of states. And as Aristide Zolberg notes in his study, the pattern appears to be movement toward military take-overs instead of brief interventions.

For purposes of comparison, then, Africa provides a number of recent military interventions which can be analyzed in order to see the ways in which military regimes come to grips with political and economic problems for the first time. Because many such interventions are only one or two years old, it may be difficult to establish patterns of rule in the initial phase, although as our contributors point out, we can see these patterns emerge as well as understand how and why the military intervenes and the problems it faces.

One particular question that clearly needs more research is that of the "contagion" or spread of the propensity to intervene. Our studies take up this problem. However, by the time many case studies have traced the spread of coups and dealt with the military as a ruling group in Sub-Saharan Africa, a number of African countries will have moved out of their initial phase of military involvement. If we are correct in suggesting that military regimes will be unstable in Africa, the second of our categories, "After the Seizure of Power: The Struggle for Stability," may give way rapidly to "Institutionalized Intervention," in which the military intervenes and then withdraws only to intervene again or in which the military itself becomes the battleground for coup and counter-coup as officers are divided by rank, generation, tribe, ideology, branch of service, or as noncommissioned personnel challenge officers.

NOTES
1. In all of Central and South America, only "Costa Rica, Uruguay, and Mexico have been free of serious military meddling in civilian affairs." Johnson, John J., "The Latin American Military," in Johnson, John J., editor, *The Role of the Military in Underdeveloped Countries*. Princeton University Press, Princeton, N.J., 1962, p. 91.

In the Middle East and North Africa a number of countries which have not had coups have a very large military involvement in politics, for example, Israel, Lebanon, Morocco, Tunisia, Saudi Arabia, and Libya. In Asia the military establishments of India, Malaysia, the Philippines, Afghanistan, and Cambodia are important in varying degrees but have not ruled their countries or appeared as overt coalition partners.

The Military in Ethiopian Politics:
Capabilities and Constraints

by Donald N. Levine

Stirred by the examples of Colonel Nasser and General Abboud in the north, embarrassed by the comparatively high standard of living in African countries to the west and south, a small band of officers sought in the closing hours of 1960 to add Ethiopia to the growing list of developing nations in which military leaders have intervened to play a decisive role in national politics. The present study attempts to set that episode and its aftermath in a broader historical and institutional context, albeit in a brief and schematic fashion. It locates the novel position of the military in contemporary Ethiopia on a plane of continuity with the Abyssinian past, and in a field of opposing and concurring forces in the present. In so doing the present study may serve not only as an effort to clarify Ethiopian realities, but also as a contribution to the comparative effort to understand the dynamics of military involvement in politics.

THE ETHIOPIAN MILITARY ORGANIZATION

The Traditional Army

Warfare has been one of the most prominent activities in the Ethiopian kingdom since its founding. The ancient kingdom at Aksum sent out a number of military expeditions in many directions—against African tribes to the north, west, and south, and twice across the Red Sea to conquer portions of Arabia. With the dissolution of the Aksumite polity around 800–1000 A.D., Ethiopian forces pushed south to invade territories of the Agau and related peoples. For two-and-a-half centuries after the ascendance of the Amhara dynasty, established by Yekuno Amlak in 1270, they carried on a long and largely successful series of campaigns against the petty Muslim states to the east. Although the *jihad* led by Ahmad Grāñ in 1527 wrought heavy destruction for many years, Ethiopian forces were routed in 1540 by an expedition of Portuguese matchlockmen and went on not only to defeat Grāñ's army but also to push back an invasion of Ottoman Turks in the north two decades later. During the three centuries which followed that victory, Ethiopian armies were preoccupied chiefly with battles against the Galla, a large tribe of pastoralists who penetrated the country from the south after Grāñ's invasion. The nineteenth century also saw a half-hearted attempt to oppose the British expedition under Napier (1868); two victorious campaigns against invading Egyptian forces in the north and a series of battles with Sudanese dervishes led by Emperor Yohannes (1872–1889); the conquest of a number of tribes in the eastern, southern, and western regions of present-day Ethiopia under Menelik (ruler of Shoa, 1865–1889, emperor of Ethiopia, 1889–1913); and a brief period of warfare against the Italians, culminating in the decisive battle of Adowa (1896).

In addition to this record of military campaigns against invaders and subject peoples, Ethiopian history is marked by chronic internecine warfare. While this was most conspicuous during the century before the coronation of Theodore II (1855) in which the absence of strong central authority promoted a condition of extreme instability, the competition and rebellion of feudal lords and the chronic antagonism between peasants and regular soldiers made civil war among groups of Amhara and Tigreans themselves a regular feature of Abyssinian history.[1] The most cursory reading of Ethiopian history cannot but support the generalization made by Ludolphus, who wrote three centuries ago: "The (Abyssinians) are a Warlike People and continually exercis'd in War . . . neither is there any respit but what is caus'd by the Winter, at what time by reason of the Inundations of the Rivers, they are forc'd to be quiet."[2]

The prominence of warfare in Ethiopian history has been matched by the conspicuous place which military culture occupies in the overall pattern of Amhara-Tigre culture. Military virtues have ranked among the highest in the Abyssinian value system; military titles have been among the most prestigious in their social hierarchy; military symbolism has provided a medium for important national traditions and a focus for a good deal of national sentiment; military statuses and procedures have influenced patterns of social organization in many ways. Indeed, in the traditional Ethiopian system, the political involvement of the military is not a phenomenon that needs to be explained; on the contrary, any distinction between the two realms is difficult to make.

In perhaps the most dramatic manifestation of this permeation of Ethiopian culture by military themes, during most of the last millennium the political capital of Ethiopia frequently took the form of an army camp. It consisted of a vast array of tents, arranged in combat-ready formation with the Emperor's tents in the center, flanked and guarded at the front and rear by officers of standard ranks with their entourages. The court would rest in one spot for a certain time—until political or military considerations dictated a move or until the local supply of firewood or food was exhausted. Then it would strike off for a new location where, on a sizable plain, a central (and often elevated) position would be staked off for the imperial tents. The rest of the population would quickly establish themselves in their accustomed positions relative to that of the emperor. The camp was so large, yet laid out so regularly, that despite its periodic movement from region to region, perceptible differences of dialect and vocabulary developed in different quarters of the mobile capital. In such a setting policies were forged, decrees promulgated, political intrigues hatched, and judicial verdicts pronounced. Even when Ethiopian emperors chose to reside for longer periods in more stable quarters, a military flavor was imparted to the capital. Military expeditions frequently originated there and high secular dignitaries bore such titles as General of the Right Flank, Commander of a Fort, and General of the Vanguard.

The armies which formed the matrix for this efflorescence of military culture in Ethiopia were not, as in Sparta, the product of careful organization and systematic development, but tended rather to be highly labile affairs. They were organized quickly, performed erratically, and dissolved in a moment. Their potency was due, not to the perfection of a specialized institution devoted to the art of warfare, but rather to the extent to which Ethiopian society as a whole was pervaded by military skills, virtues, and ambitions. For while the Ethiopian Army was neither trained nor disciplined, it could count on a number of cultural factors to produce an effective soldiery.

(1) Observers of many centuries have commented on the extraordinary physical capacities of the Abyssinian people. As a rule thin, light, almost frail in appearance, the Abyssinian soldier is nevertheless noted for great endurance—he can climb mountains with ease, march rapidly for long distances under heavy pack with light rations, and can sleep on a rock.

(2) Knowledge of how to use whatever weapons were available in

a given century and region was widely diffused throughout the male population. Men saw and practiced arms from early childhood. Possession of arms of some sort—formerly a spear, during the last century increasingly a rifle—has been considered a normal mark of manhood.

(3) A cult of masculinity was highly developed in Abyssinia and conceived specifically in terms of military prowess.[3] To be a man was to be a killer, tireless on the warpath and fearless in battle. The prospect of acquiring prestige through trophies collected from murdered enemies was a powerful incentive.

(4) The prospect of acquiring booty was another powerful incentive. The norms of combat in Abyssinia included wanton expropriation of conquered peoples. Cattle, grain, arms, and sometimes slaves were among the items to be gained.

(5) Success in military activity was the key route to social mobility. Outstanding achievement at arms brought a man honors, favors, and political appointments. Men with any ambition at all—and most had dreams of rising high at some time in their society, which provided some opportunity for and much talk about upward mobility—were thus motivated to seek occasions for combat.

(6) Personal loyalties, finally, played an important part in many cases—not the horizontal loyalty to comrades, which has been stressed in sociological studies of modern armies, but vertical loyalties to one's chief or patron.[4] Although service under a master was voluntary and was frequently discontinued when the leader's fortunes waned, so long as the leader was successful and reasonably effective in rewarding and supplying his followers—and in some cases even when he was not—a sense of being "his man" and wanting to be brave for him was another factor that motivated Abyssinians to do well in battle.

As this last consideration suggests, historical Ethiopian armies consisted of a number of individual leaders—the Emperor and the governors of provinces—and the fluctuating numbers of troops under their personal command. These troops were of three kinds. First, each "big man" had a standing corps of soldiers, armed retainers who lived near his quarters. Such men served their master for the security and comfort that came from living near a seat of power and at his expense. Second, there were men whose rights to the use of certain land entailed the obligation to serve some designated ruler for two or three months during the year—a kind of corvée labor in the form of military service. Third, there was the mass levy in time of emergency. Such troops were recruited by sending out a proclamation, and bringing to bear various formal and informal sanctions against those qualified males who failed to turn out. Delinquents in Menelik's day were punished by confiscation of goods, whipping, and imprisonment. One of his proclamations states that "if an eligible man remains at home, let him be called by the name of woman, and let his wife take possession of all his wealth and become head of the household."[5]

It was thus assumed in Abyssinia that every able-bodied adult male who did not belong to the clergy was willing and able to be an effective soldier. This assumption produced bewilderment and dismay when acted on in warfare against the Italians in 1935–1936, but until then it had been sound enough for Abyssinian purposes. The existence of a ready supply of capable soldiers enabled the traditional military system to function on a highly individualistic basis. Each soldier was responsible for procuring weapons, either from his own resources or through arrangements with his leader (although by the time of Menelik soldiers were typically issued rifles). He was expected to acquire the skills needed to use them on his own; there was no provision for collective training procedures of any sort. He was likewise expected to arrange his own logistics; he either walked to battle or else brought his own mule, arranged for his own sleeping quarters, brought his own food supply and supplemented it by preying on local peasants as he went, and brought along his wife or maidservant to prepare his food. Finally, each soldier was his own master in battle. The Abyssinian fighting unit was not the squad or platoon, but the individual combatant, who sized up the situation as he went along, chose his own time and place to close with the enemy, and chose the objects for his personal attack.[6]

Viewed as a collectivity, however, the traditional Abyssinian army appears to have been a comparatively unstable and inefficient organization. Troops moved into battle in a disorderly manner. They were not accustomed to persevering in battle; at the first sign of defeat, mass retreat was not unusual. When their leaders faltered, or failed to provide for them properly, or appeared to be heading for failure, Abyssinian soldiers often deserted en masse and went over to the other side. They were as quick to abandon the military role as they had been eager to assume it; barely had the din of battle ceased when they set about pursuing their favorite pursuits of civil litigation, plotting political intrigue, and caring for their home estates.

Even when fighting at their best, moreover, the Abyssinian soldiery did not form an efficient military force. Their standard tactics were to engage in massive sudden attacks in an effort to envelop and confound the enemy; the alternatives were victory or retreat. The more subtle maneuvers of guerrilla warfare and the taking of cover were tactics that conflicted with their ethic of impetuous, fearless aggression. Because of this "unreasoning offensive spirit," an Italian officer wrote in 1937, Ethiopian troops were easy to defeat by a disciplined modern army.[7] It was clear to Haile Selassie from the beginning of his reign that modern forms of organization as well as military technology were indispensable if Ethiopia were to continue to be a proud power.

Modernization of the Armed Forces

The modernization of Ethiopian military forces was prefigured by the Portuguese mission of the sixteenth century, which brought the first supply of firearms into the country and taught Abyssinian soldiers how to use the new weapons. While additional supplies of modern weapons filtered into the country during succeeding centuries, substantial modernization of Ethiopian military technology did not occur until the late nineteenth century. The turning point was perhaps the defeat of the Egyptian forces by Yohannes: 20,000 Remington rifles were taken after the Battle of Gura (1876) alone. Subsequently, Menelik imported large quantities of rifles and ammunition and some artillery from France and Italy, an effort aided by the competition between these two powers to win his friendship. With the establishment of Italian and French ports on the Red Sea and Gulf of Aden, Menelik's needs for weaponry were filled by a lively arms trade. By the time of the battle of Adowa in 1896 the armies of Menelik and his generals possessed an estimated 100,000 rifles and 40 cannon.[8] Menelik also employed French officers to train some of his personal troops.

A more serious attempt to impart modern military training to Ethiopian soldiers was carried out during the regency and reign of Haile Selassie, who sent a number of Ethiopian officers to the St. Cyr Military Academy in France in the 1920's. He also brought to Ethiopia in 1929 a military mission from Belgium that trained his Imperial Bodyguard for half a dozen years. Swiss and Belgian officers were sent to train the troops in his province of Hararge. In 1934 he established a Military Academy at Holeta, initially under Swedish management, 30 miles from Addis Ababa.

Haile Selassie's program of military modernization was barely launched, of course, before the Ethiopian Army was put to a shattering test. When the war with Italy broke out, only an insignificant number of Ethiopians could be said to have been modern soldiers commanded by trained officers. The vast majority of the troops were traditional soldiery, armed with spears or old-fashioned rifles and led by men who held their positions as old nobles or provincial governors rather than as professional officers. The modern ideas of strategy adopted by the Emperor at the instigation of European military advisers only confused and undermined the confidence of the old-time commanders and their armies.

By the time Ethiopian troops were fully defeated by the Italians in 1937, however, important lessons had been painfully learned. Ethiopian soldiers adapted themselves to guerrilla techniques and, through constant harassment of Italian troops in well-chosen times and places, so undermined Italian morale that reconquest of the country was relatively speedy in 1941.[9] The need for modern training as well as weapons had been seen clearly by many men other than the small circle of European-oriented leaders at the top. After the liberation the government moved posthaste to replace the traditional system with a standing modern Army. The Emperor concentrated the responsibility for military activity in a national Ministry of War (later changed to Defense). The strength of the traditional war lords in the provinces had been greatly depleted by the losses of the war, and the Emperor effectively eliminated their potential for a comeback by depriving them of the right to appropriate local revenues, the foundation of their capacity to acquire soldiers in the past. The postwar development of the Ethiopian military forces may be traced in three stages, paralleling the three phases of political involvement by the military to be discussed in the next section.

I. *1942–1950:* The years following the liberation were marked by rapid development of modern-trained troops primarily under British auspices. Under a convention signed in 1942 the British agreed to provide at their own cost a mission "for the purpose of raising, organizing, and training the Ethiopian Army." They had begun such training in Khartoum in 1940, and proceeded to equip and instruct ten infantry battalions, a regiment of pack artillery, an armored car regiment, and engineer and signal services. The battalions thus readied were stationed at key points around the country and played an important role in maintaining internal security during the unstable decade which followed liberation. In addition, the Emperor revived and trained his Imperial Bodyguard under the command of Ethiopian officers who had attended the Holeta Academy before the war and matured during the campaign of liberation. As an indication of the seriousness with which the government took this military build-up, in addition to the resources contributed by the British, Ethiopian expenditures for the Ministry of War and Imperial Bodyguard alone—that is, excluding expenditures for police and other security services—amounted to 38 per cent of the total national budget in 1943–1944. The following year it dropped to about 25 per cent (although the absolute figures remained about the same) and remained approximately at that level the rest of the decade—in each year constituting the largest single item on the national budget.[10]

In addition to the forces trained by the British mission and those of the Emperor's Bodyguard, another army was set up in Ethiopia during this period. In order to absorb and disarm the relatively large numbers of armed patriot bands which were roaming the country as outlaws after the liberation, a loose Territorial Army was organized. In contrast to the new standing national forces, men entering this Army were not given rifles but rather were enlisted only if they already possessed rifles. This Territorial Army thus served to check postwar unemployment and brigandage. By the close of this period, most of its members had been absorbed into the regular Army or else into the newly formed National Police.

II. *1951–1960:* This period was marked by the replacement of British influence by a number of other foreign military missions, the expansion and diversification of the military forces, the introduction of substantial American aid, and the first participation of Ethiopian forces in an international military campaign.

The British mission began to withdraw during the late 1940's and left Ethiopia altogether in 1951. In an effort to reduce British influence in this area, the Ethiopian government had brought in Swedish military advisers and instructors as early as 1946. In 1953 a United States military assistance group came to Ethiopia to help train and equip various branches of the security forces. Swedish officers were brought to train the new Air Force, Norwegians for the fledgling Navy. Three cadet groups were taken successively through three-year training programs, in which Swedish officers also played a part. In 1958 a military mission from India came to set up and manage the new Military Academy at Harar. Israeli officers have also served as instructors in various sectors of the military establishment, and Japanese instructors were imported to train security personnel. Ethiopian officers were also sent abroad for training in a variety of countries, including the United States, England, and Yugoslavia.

In 1951 the Kagnew Battalion, formed of crack troops selected from the Imperial Bodyguard, was sent to Korea to fight with the United Nations forces as part of the U.S. Seventh Division. Altogether, three battalions were sent prior to the cease-fire, a total of about 5,000 men; and additional battalions were stationed there following the truce. In appreciation of Ethiopia's contribution to the Korean campaign and in exchange for rights to set up a U.S. army base at Asmara, Ethiopia received a substantial amount of military assistance. The amount given to Ethiopia from 1950 to 1965 exceeds U.S. $91 million, approximately half of the amount of military aid given in all Africa during this period.

III. *1961–1966:* In the past half-dozen years no notable changes took place in the patterns of modernization, but Ethiopian troops were provided with three important occasions for active duty and thereby increased the general prominence of the professional Army in Ethiopian life. Ethiopia was among the first countries to send forces to the Congo; over 3,000 Ethiopian troops and half an air squadron participated in the United Nations military action there. Closer to home, skirmishes in the vicinity of the Somali border have occasioned a number of military reprisals and attacks, and the stationing of larger numbers of troops on the alert in the Ogaden. (The Somali danger also resulted in Ethiopia's first defense pact, with Kenya, in December, 1963.) Internally, the rebellion of the Imperial Bodyguard in December, 1960, led to an engagement in which the regular Army and the Air Force quashed the rebels after a day of heavy fighting. In the wake of this revolt, the officer corps of the Bodyguard was completely dismantled, and a new Imperial Bodyguard was reconstituted with fresh troops and officers from the Army and a new period of training under Indian officers.

The Military Today: Organization, Size, Recruitment, and Training

The Emperor remains the Commander-in-Chief of the Armed Forces of Ethiopia and intervenes authoritatively in all important decisions. Theoretically he is advised by a National Defense Council, about which little is known. Reporting directly to him are the Commander of the Imperial Bodyguard; the Minister of Interior, under whom are the Chief of Police and the Chief of Security; his own private intelligence networks; and the Minister of Defense. The latter commands the Chief of Staff, under whom are the Commanders of the Army, Navy, and Air Force; though in practice all of these officers also report directly to the Emperor.

The Imperial Bodyguard today consists of about 6,000 men, organized in 9 infantry battalions. The regular Army consists of about 24,000 men, including 23 infantry and 4 artillery battalions, an armored squadron, and an airborne rifle company. The Air Force numbers some 1,300 men, and includes a squadron of F-86 jet fighters, 5 T-33 jet trainers, and a transport squadron with DC-3's and C-47's (all American made), as well as 18 piston-engined Swedish Saab-91 training craft and 2 squadrons of Saab-17 light bombers. The Navy has about 3,000 men, and includes 5 95-foot U.S. coastal patrol boats, 2 Yugoslav motor torpedo boats, and an eighteen-year-old reconverted seaplane tender outfitted as a patrol-boat tender, training vessel, and imperial flagship. There are approximately 30,000 men in the National Police force distributed throughout the country.[11] Since 1960 the Territorial Army has been reorganized. Little is known about it, though it is said to be concentrated in Shoa province at locations not too far from Addis Ababa.

Noncommissioned personnel have been recruited into the Ethiopian security forces on a purely voluntary basis, although unconfirmed rumors state that vagrants in the cities are sometimes conscripted into military service as they have been for service in the gold mines. They come primarily from three sources: patriots who fought in the underground during the Italian Occupation; rural youths who are dissatisfied with their lot and interested in the opportunities, adventure, and "manly" life of the soldier; and the unemployed of the cities, including numerous school dropouts.

The older generation of Army officers likewise enlisted voluntarily, as have most, if not all, of the Air Force cadets. The older officers include a small group who received some modern training before the Italian War; a group of officers of field-grade level who served with the patriot forces and are relatively untrained; and a group who were in exile with the Emperor during the Occupation and received some training at French or British hands during the war years. By contrast, the postwar cadres of officers in the Bodyguard, Navy, and (since 1957) Army have been recruited largely through conscription for life-time service, an action which has frequently resulted in considerable bitterness over their being deprived of the possibility of civilian careers.

These cadres have been hand-picked from the cream of secondary school seniors and first-year college students.

In terms of ethnic composition, the enlisted men consist primarily of Amhara, with some Tigreans and a heavy admixture of Galla. At the commissioned level, the proportion of Tigreans is higher and that of Galla lower. A survey of the cadets in the Harar Military Academy in 1959–1960 revealed the following ethnic distribution: Amhara, 53 per cent; Tigrean, 26 per cent; Aderi (native of Harar) and Galla, 8 per cent; no reply, 13 per cent. With respect to the socioeconomic class of their families, the same cadets responded as follows: upper class, 11 per cent; middle class, 53 per cent; "poor" or lower class, 21 per cent; peasant class, 3 per cent; no reply, 13 per cent.

Five schools are now devoted to the training of military personnel: the Infantry School at Holeta, the Air Force School at Debra Zeit, the Naval Cadets' School at Massawa, the Abba Dina Police College in Addis Ababa, and the Haile Selassie I Military Academy at Harar. All but the first of these are geared primarily to the training of commissioned officers, and accept only well-qualified secondary-school graduates in their programs. They are educational institutions in a broad sense, including in their curricula a variety of academic and practical subjects in addition to the strictly military and technical ones. The Abba Dina Police College, for example, which is in the process of expanding from a two-year to a three-year program, provides courses in law for its students, while cadets at the Harar Academy take courses in English literature. In addition to their substantive content, these training programs have three general educational objectives: the development of a loyalty to the nation that transcends loyalty to particular ethnic groups; the substitution of an ethic of professional competence for the old-fashioned military ethic of naive martial enthusiasm and wanton bravery; and the substitution of an ethic of professional duty for the old-fashioned ethic of political ambition through military service.

THE ETHIOPIAN POLITICAL SYSTEM

Contemporary Political Structure

THE salient features of Ethiopia's political structure are generally well-known and need only be briefly reviewed here. Ethiopia is governed by a monarch whose theoretically absolute powers are legitimated both by ancient traditions and by a written Constitution (1955), which asserts that "By virtue of His Imperial Blood, as well as by the anointing which He has received, the person of the Emperor is sacred, His dignity is inviolable and His power is indisputable." Haile Selassie, the present incumbent, has worked steadfastly to consolidate and assert the full imperial power ever since his emergence on the national scene as Regent following a coup d'état in 1916. In the prewar years, he attained this goal by building up his military strength to the point where he was stronger than any of the semi-autonomous feudal lords who might oppose him. Their power was decisively undercut in 1942, when the establishment of a national Ministry of Finance eliminated their rights to collect revenues, and when all provincial governmental functions were made subordinate to centralized Ministries of Interior and Justice. At the same time he constructed an elaborate edifice of national administration, including sixteen ministries; a number of independent agencies performing various developmental functions, like the Imperial Highway Authority and the Imperial Board of Telecommunications; and a number of coordinating bodies under the Council of Ministers, such as the National Coffee Board and the Economic and Technical Assistance Board.

Over all these administrative organs the Emperor's authority has remained supreme. While the burgeoning of this new governmental apparatus created new sources of power and hence potential opposition, the present Emperor has managed to secure the minimal loyalty of most members of the administration through a subtly graded system of economic and social rewards, and to forestall threatening coalescenses of interest through a multiplex surveillance network and a skillfully applied policy of *divide et impera*.

Haile Selassie has also established a Parliament in Ethiopia. The first Parliament, set up in 1931, consisted of a Senate whose members were appointed by the Emperor, and a Chamber of Deputies who were chosen by the nobility and local chiefs. Since the new Constitution of 1955, members of the Chamber of Deputies have been elected by universal suffrage; such elections were held in 1957, 1961, and 1965. The Parliament exists primarily as a deliberative body, since legislative power remains essentially in the hands of the Emperor. The Ethiopian Parliament convenes annually, but because the proceedings of Parliament are not regularly covered by the Press or published entire in any form, it is difficult to determine exactly what happens in its deliberations.

The fourteen provincial governments are headed either by governor-generals, or by deputy governor-generals, appointed by the Emperor and receiving salaries through the Ministry of Interior. Under them are numerous district governors and subdistrict governors. All these officials are placed in lines of command emanating from the Emperor and the national Ministry of Interior, although in outlying districts the authority of Addis Ababa has not penetrated very deeply and these men are often members of local families long important in the area. This system of provincial administration is paralleled by a complex judicial system, which includes seven appellate levels culminating in the Emperor's private court. In addition, each provincial and subprovincial center includes a contingent from the National Police force.

Stability of the Present Regime

Although the present regime has attained a degree of autocratic control previously unknown in Ethiopian history, and although natural processes of social change at work in the country have introduced many new sources of tension, it has been characterized by a basic continuity and stability remarkable for a part of the world where convulsive change of government has been frequent in recent decades. As an indication of the magnitude of the present Emperor's political achievement consider that his predecessor, Lijj Iyasu, had far better genealogical claims to the throne, but was overturned after only three years in the imperial office. Haile Selassie, however, has played the dominant role in shaping the fate of Ethiopia for virtually half a century now. In addition to his unusual manipulative talents, the durability of his regime may be attributed to the following factors.

(1) Sanctity of the Imperial office is an ancient theme in Abyssinian tradition. So long as the Emperor remains true to the Ethiopian Orthodox Church—it was Lijj Iyasu's alleged conversion to Islam that hastened his downfall—he is endowed with a sacred aura that rests on three considerations: his membership in a royal line hallowed by alleged descent from King Solomon; his anointment at the hands of the archbishop of the Church; and his role as protector and defender of the Church.

(2) The centralization of military power in Addis Ababa before and after the Italian Occupation gave Haile Selassie the force with which to back up his claims to legitimate authority. The two dozen years of systematic acquisition and purchase of arms by Menelik after 1878 de-

cisively shifted the balance of military power in the empire to the central province of Shoa. The modernization of Haile Selassie's troops in the 1920's and early 1930's increased the extent of Shoan superiority, and the establishment of the British-trained regular Army following liberation, together with the reconstituted Bodyguard and National Police system, definitively raised the might of Addis Ababa far above that which any potential provincial opponent could muster.

(3) The authoritarian ethos characteristic of Abyssinian culture has favored a state of mind which cheerfully relegates the responsibility for decisions concerning the public realm to the highest authorities, and which discourages the open expression of criticism of such authorities. This ethos is supported both by Biblical notion that it is immoral to disobey one's superior and the secular argument that human affairs and social relations are headed for trouble in the absence of strong authoritarian leadership.[12] Thus, numerous Ethiopians who have had strong personal grievances against the Emperor or serious disagreements with some of his policies have refrained from criticizing him publicly in any way and have consistently shown him the greatest deference.

(4) The pursuit of interest on an individualistic basis has worked to support the present regime and Haile Selassie has deliberately sought to perpetuate it for that purpose. The traditional social system of Abyssinia encourages the pursuit of individual, not collective, ambition. It is lacking in mechanisms by which individuals can associate in the pursuit of collective interests. There are no fixed corporate structures, either in the kinship system or on a territorial or civic basis, which might channel the pursuit of common interests. There are almost no traditional patterns for cooperation beyond the reciprocal arrangements for attaining such restricted goals as the construction of a roof or the repair of a church.[13] The Abyssinians are sociologically unequipped for banding together to confront some authority with common demands. Their system promotes, rather, the pursuit of individual advantage by means of winning favor of some authority. Ethiopians today have therefore been almost—but not quite—as little disposed to insist on forming associations for the articulation and aggregation of interests as the Emperor has been disposed to permit the formation of such associations. Labor unions were not allowed in Ethiopia until 1963, professional associations have been discouraged, and political parties are still not permitted. The combination of repressive policies

on the part of the government and the individualistic character of the populace has resulted in the absence of organized groups which could threaten the regime in any way.

(5) The arrangement of marriages in order to promote political harmony has been a stabilizing technique used with great effectiveness throughout the present regime, beginning with Haile Selassie's own marriage to the daughter of an important Galla chieftain before he came to power. Haile Selassie has brought nearly all of the great, politically problematic families in the country into his fold by marrying one of their members to one of his children or other relatives.

(6) The symbolic adequacy and instrumental effectiveness of Haile Selassie's regime must also be credited for contributing significantly to its durability. While all segments of the population know areas of frustration for which they hold him responsible, all of them are able to identify with him in some respect and to remember some of his policies from which they have benefited. While he has undermined the power of the old nobility, he gratifies them by retaining much of the old court symbolism and has rewarded many of them with appointments to the Senate and in the provincial administration. While he has undermined the power of the clergy to some extent and has been a primary agent of secularization in the country, he remains steadfast in his adherence to the basic traditions of the Orthodox Church, has won its independence from the partriarchate at Alexandria, and has handsomely rewarded the highest dignitaries of the Church. While he has antagonized the Abyssinian peasantry in various ways—by building up Addis Ababa at the expense of the provinces, by showing favoritism of various sorts, by maintaining what some feel to be a repressive political system, by introducing alien ways—he has won their everlasting gratitude by symbolizing the independence of Ethiopia from European rule, by freeing them from the traditional necessity of paying indefinite amounts of tribute and corvée labor to exploitative local lords, and by bringing such benefits as roads and medical centers into some outlying regions. While he has kept the highest government officials in a state of anxiety and overdependence through the high-handed use of his authority, he has given them much of what prestige and income they possess and has increased the national prestige of Ethiopia so that they are benefited in many ways. While his behavior toward the modern-educated has often offended their dignity and while his policies have been (privately) criticized by them as illiberal and insufficiently pro-

gressive, he has also been identified as responsible for introducing modern education into Ethiopia and for giving them what facilities and rewards they now possess. Although to numerous ethnic and regional groups throughout the country he symbolizes the continuance of Shoan dominance under which many chafe, he gratifies them by virtue of the majesty of being an *Emperor* and by such improvements as increased security in the provinces and the rudimentary signs of better living standards. To all parts of the population, finally, his diplomatic success in capturing an important place in the leadership of the pan-African movement during the past decade has been a conspicuous source of support for the regime.

THE POLITICAL CAPABILITY OF THE MILITARY

ACUTELY aware of the age-old connection between military activity and political ambition in Ethiopia, Emperor Haile Selassie has taken pains to instill in his professional military forces the idea that they are to be guided solely by an ethic of duty and to refrain from getting involved in the political realm. The heading of every issue of the official Bodyguard newspaper has carried the injunction: "The soldier's work is to follow orders, not to engage in politics." The lesson was repeated at all levels: when General Mengistu Neway, the late Commander of the Imperial Bodyguard, was on a tour of the country with the Emperor in the 1950's, he was struck by the hunger and poverty of the people in a certain region and asked if something could not be done about it. The Emperor is said to have replied, "What's this? Meddling in politics? That is none of your business."

Significant as this question of the degree of *interest* in a political role may be, it does not afford so revealing a category for dealing with the political involvement of the military as does the category of political *capability*. For although interest may be high, the capability may be so low as to preclude the possibility of such involvement; conversely, even though such interest may be low, a military organization with a high degree of political capability may be pressured by societal strains and the flow of events into playing an important political role. In analyzing the elements of such capability, four variables seem to be of obvious significance: the economic and cultural resources of the military; their politically relevant value orientations; their position in the social structure; and their internal organization.

Economic and Cultural Resources

As we have seen, military expenditures have constituted the largest single item in the national budget ever since the liberation. During the past seven years expenses for the Armed Forces have averaged about 17 per cent of the budget. (Figures for the Police and security departments are not available.) In 1963 this amounted to approximately US $18 million. While not large in absolute terms, it represents the largest defense outlay of any country in Sub-Saharan Africa except South Africa and, in the past few years, Ghana and Nigeria.[14]

The income of the higher-ranking officers has been impressive by Ethiopian standards. They have received substantial salaries, free housing, free cars, and servants and retainers drawn from the ranks. In many cases their income is supplemented by rents from land holdings in the provinces and urban real estate, and at times by personal gifts presented directly by the Emperor. Many officers in the Air Force in particular have been recipients of royal gifts in the form of land and other privileges. Lower-ranking officers have complained of income insufficient to meet their minimal needs, and the low income of enlisted men has been a source of acute dissatisfaction for many years.

Collectively, the military possess a modest proportion of the country's modern facilities. They have their own engineers and roadbuilders, if not of the best quality; their own hospitals and doctors, if not the most effective. They operate at least three internal newspapers, and the Imperial Bodyguard operated a radio station in the 1950's until it was closed down because of political pressures.

The postwar generation of officers represent a significant proportion—probably no fewer than 10 to 12 per cent—of all Ethiopians who have received modern education beyond the secondary level. Many of them pursue additional education on their own, those in Addis Ababa attending extension courses at the University.

Perhaps the most conspicuous cultural resource of the military is their primary role in the development of a secular national culture in postwar Ethiopia. Their soccer teams have helped to focus attention on national sports. Their Olympic champion Sergeant Abebe Bikila, two-time marathon winner, has been a major national hero and the focus of much national pride—and was the only Ethiopian other than the Emperor to be greeted by cheering crowds at the airport. In music, the military services have not only been the principal source of performing musicians in the modernizing sector—Army, Bodyguard, and Police have each maintained popular dance bands, and the Police have pioneered with a symphony orchestra—but have created distinctive Ethiopian tunes which have become popular with their countrymen. These and similar innovations have been fostered by their self-confident realization that in Ethiopia the military is the only institution that is simultaneously traditional, modern, and national; that they have a natural mission, as it were, to procreate the new national culture of modernizing Ethiopia.

Value Orientations

Although not much reliable information is available on the subject, it may be suggested with some confidence that, after national independence, technical modernization and social welfare are the primary values toward which most Ethiopian military officers are oriented. No longer are Ethiopian officers oriented in terms of defending the Church: religious issues have receded, and a good many military officers have become atheists, especially those trained under the Indian military mission. Nor are they likely to pursue partisan ethnic causes; a real and vital sense of common nationality is perhaps stronger among the military than elsewhere in the country. They favor technical modernization because their experience of modern technology has convinced them that it can only be useful for the nation, and those who have been abroad for training or active duty are particularly eager to have their country "catch up" with what they have seen elsewhere. They favor social welfare because most of them stem from humble families, and they feel a patriotic inclination to see the lot of their countrymen improved. While they do not reject the authoritarian ethos of Abyssinia, they do reject the traditional pattern in which a privileged few live at the expense of a relatively impoverished many. Many of them have objected to what they considered the corruption of the present regime and its "parasites," and to the extent to which the Emperor was using his authority arbitrarily and unproductively. While most of them probably felt loyal to Haile Selassie in the years just after liberation, throughout the 1950's increasing numbers of officers were becoming alienated from his regime. To some extent this reflected grievances over salary on the part of lower-ranking officers and enlisted men; to some extent it meant a growing political consciousness. As one former officer of the Bodyguard recollected:

> Around the time of the Korean War a number of us officers in the Imperial Bodyguard began to talk about things that were bothering us. We observed the many oppressions in our country. We understood that it was not right for Ethiopians to live in subjugation under the power of one man. We saw that justice was destroyed and that everything was done by lies. Inspired by the spirit of nationalism, we therefore began to express opposition in conversations among ourselves.

Finally, most of them have not the slightest interest in an aggressive, expansionist nationalism, although some of the older officers have been advocates of a "preventive war" against Somalia. In recent years they have developed a keen interest in African politics and a sympathetic orientation toward the pan-African movement.

Position in Society

The status of the military in Abyssinian society was marked by three characteristics: lack of isolation of the military from civilian society; public appreciation of the values embodied by the military; public dislike of the predatory aspects of military behavior. In modified form, these characteristics are still in evidence today.

Although because of their special training centers and chains of command the military are today far more separated from the rest of society than before the war, they appear to remain in more intimate contact with civilian society than is true, say, of the American military. Most members of the forces stationed in Addis Ababa live, not in barracks, but in private quarters among the civilian populations. Military officers interact a good deal with civilians of high status at parties, dances, weddings, and funerals. Army officers are often related to civilian officials by blood or marriage. They mingle with civilian students at extension courses of the University. The postwar-trained officers typically retain contacts with their former fellow students from secondary school days.

With respect to their attitudes toward the military, the civilian part of the population is ambivalent. The negative side of their attitude does not rest, as in some democratic societies, on an ideological distrust of the military because of their association with "militarism" and anti-democratic tendencies. On the contrary, at the ideological level Ethiopian society is, if anything, promilitary. Rather, the dislike of the military has to do with a sense of their being parasites on the people. Traditionally, this negative attitude arose as a reaction against the forces' quartering and pillage associated with soldiers on the warpath. Haile Selassie sought to overcome that opprobrium in the Italian campaign by insisting that civilians be reimbursed for anything that soldiers needed to take from them. It has a contemporary counterpart, however, in the idea that the military today are doing nothing to develop the country, that they just sit around and eat up the results of the hard work of others. The arrogant behavior of many veterans of the Korean campaign in the bars and cafés of Addis Ababa in the mid-1950's also exacerbated civilian feelings.

In two important respects, on the other hand, the military are objects of the highest admiration and appreciation. They are appreciated for defending the country's territorial integrity and political independence, matters about which Abyssinians feel very strongly. They represent, moreover, the style of life and the virtues connected with virile masculinity, an ethic which remains of some importance in Ethiopian culture. The generally high esteem which the military enjoys because of these reasons, the appreciation of their contribution to the secular national culture, and the tradition of military involvement in politics suggests that the assumption of greater responsibility for national development by the military would not be regarded by the public as an unpleasant prospect, but might be welcomed as an opportunity for the military to stop sitting around and start doing something substantial for the country.

Some characteristics of the specific relations between the military and other elites in Ethiopian society can be noted. The regular clergy continue to have the same supportive attitude they have always had toward Ethiopian military endeavors. The two establishments are acknowledged partners in maintaining civil order. When the Army and Air Force were putting down the rebellion in 1960, one of their early actions was to drop leaflets containing a statement by the Archbishop that those who aided the rebels would be excommunicated. So long as there was broad agreement between the military and ecclesiastical leaders with respect to policies pursued, the support of the latter could probably be assumed and would be of some import. While most members of the Church hierarchy oppose many aspects of modernization, they have probably been most sympathetic to such modernization as has taken place under military auspices. In the event that the military becomes militantly secular, however, the Church might become alienated from them, a development that would, in turn, canalize opinion in crucial provinces against the military. Insofar as the Territorial Army is a force to reckon with, it can be considered much more closely tied to the traditional Church.

The civilian government officials live in a state of considerable anxiety over the prospect of being displaced by the military. One of the ministers most sensitive to this possiblity, the late Makonnen Habtewold, was instrumental in having the Emperor make certain high level changes in military personnel and close down the Imperial Bodyguard radio station in the 1950's because he felt that the popularity of the Imperial Bodyguard and the stimulation of their political ambitions were reaching a dangerous point. Because of their fear of displacement, some of the civilian bureaucrats might be inclined to join with the church in the event of a Church-Army showdown.

The students and young intellectuals combine appreciation of the military's potential for modernizing the country with fear of the illiberal tendencies that might be associated with military rule. Most recently students have carried on a demonstration in Addis Ababa protesting "police brutality" in the suppression of an earlier student demonstration. But for the most part students and other youth appear sympathetic to the idea of universal military service, an idea currently promoted by some military men as a means of increasing civilian-military harmony.

Inner Solidarity

Aware of the relatively high esteem of the military in Ethiopia and of its potential, through possession of modern technology and aspirations as well as its monopoly of the means of violence, for radical intrusion into the political process, Haile Selassie has pursued a policy of checking, balancing, and dividing the Armed Forces internally since their establishment as a standing professional force. To the effect of his deliberately divisive policies must be added a number of tensions within the military which have emerged spontaneously.

Within the Army, the main axes of cleavage among the officers have been those dividing the postwar cadres from the older groups. These tensions have been partly those of a generational nature, partly reflections of ideological differences between the more progressive-minded of both groups and the conservatives among the older group. Differences in outlook stemming from the variety of national traditions —French, British, and American—which have influenced their training have compounded the cleavages to some extent. Finally, the alleged permeation of the military ranks with government informers, especially in recent years, has worked to sow widespread suspicion among the officers and to inhibit communication to a considerable extent.

Unlike the Army, the differences among officers in the Imperial Bodyguard were not so pronounced. The bulk of Bodyguard officers stemmed from the postwar period. They developed a morale and esprit, stimulated partly by their privileged training, uniforms, and other perquisites, including a handsome officers' club, which was a center for numerous cultural as well as social and athletic activities. These conditions led them to take a more sanguine view of the overall solidarity of the military than ever existed. In 1960, before the coup, a number of Bodyguard officers said in private conversation: "If and when the time for action comes, all of the Armed Forces will rise as one man."

The somewhat privileged status and perquisites of the Bodyguard had the additional effect, however, of arousing a good deal of envy among the Army officers. They were particularly envious because the officers and troops who went to Korea were nearly exclusively drawn from the Bodyguard ranks. Despite occasional friendships among individual officers from both forces, the relationship between Army and Bodyguard as a whole was colored by a significant amount of antagonism.

I do not have sufficient information to comment securely upon the internal solidarity of the Air Force, Navy, and Police, or of their relationships with the other Armed Forces. It is likely that morale is relatively high among the Air Force officers, since all of them represent the postwar generations and derive satisfactions and prestige from their familiarity with aeronautic technology. But the overarching reality in all these services is the fear of informants and mutual suspiciousness that decisively inhibits the development of the kind of solidarity that marked the Imperial Bodyguard in the 1950's.

PATTERNS AND SOURCES OF POLITICAL INVOLVEMENT

ETHIOPIAN military personnel have become directly involved in the input and output functions of government in four distinct ways in the postwar years: military personnel have been assigned to governmental positions; military activity has been a means of competing for power;

one group among the military forces seized control of the government in a short-lived coup d'état; and one group of the military created a precedent for public political expression in an unusual instance of institutional interest articulation. Broadly speaking, these types of involvement can be related to specific patterns of societal development and tension in the three periods following liberation which were described above.

1942–1950: Traditional Patterns of Political Involvement

The fusion of military and political roles was manifest in two ways in Abyssinian society. First, military activity was the key route to attain political power, both for the ambitious commoner or young man who sought to be rewarded by his lord with a political appointment of some sort, and for the ambitious lord whose fortunes vis-à-vis other lords depended to a large extent on the size and effectiveness of the army he could muster. Second, administrative, fiscal, and judicial functions were normally performed by men who were also military leaders and bore military titles.

With the reforms of 1942 Haile Selassie differentiated the two realms once and for all. Provincial lords were deprived of their private armies, and the civilian functions of government were bestowed upon specifically designated civilian officials just as the military functions devolved upon professional soldiers. But the transition was not completed overnight, and it is not difficult to discern in the new era what might be called modes of political involvement of the military that are cognate with the older patterns.

In 1943 a rebellion broke out in Tigre Province. The rebels blockaded the northern main road and stormed the provincial capital of Makalle. Battalions of the Territorial Army were sent up to no avail, and then two battalions of the British-trained regular Army were dispatched. The rebels were defeated after heavy fighting, and the bombing of the Makalle market by British planes. Earlier in the year, two Army battalions had been sent to contain hostilities in Hararge Province instigated by a group of Somalis. From the viewpoint of a modernized polity, these two incidents would be counted simply as instances of the normal military function of maintaining domestic security. But it had not been more than a dozen or so years earlier that the imperial forces were competing on a somewhat more equal basis with rebellious forces in the west and north. One scion of the old Tigre dynasty was associated, if only circumstantially, with the 1943 rebellion, and thus the military action against the Tigre rebels bears a sociological family resemblance to the old power struggles between an emperor and a dissident feudal lord. A more benign pattern of military involvement was that of appointing military personnel to governmental posts. By this is meant not merely that many of the postwar bureaucratic officials held the old military titles like *Dejazmatch* (Commander of the Gate) and *Balambaras* (Commander of a Fort). By 1942, these titles had become purely honorific, and the higher military ranks were represented by European terms. In addition to this traditionalistic usage, however, the Emperor appointed a number of men who were professional soldiers in the new Army to administrative posts in the government. This practice was continued through the 1950's. Among the most important appointments of this sort may be cited an acting Minister of Interior; the (late) minister of National Community Development, who had formerly been Commander of the Imperial Bodyguard; the Minister of Defense; and the governors of four of the largest and wealthiest provinces: Eritrea, Hararge, Kaffa, and Sidamo. Even though appointed to civilian posts, such men retained their professional military titles.

1951–1960: Modernizing Tensions and Political Involvement

The decade of the 1950's was marked by relative calm with respect to the provinces. Although tensions in Eritrea (which was federated with Ethiopia in 1952), the Somali area, and elsewhere existed below the surface, no attempt was made to gain power through provincial insurrection.

A new source of tension, however, appeared as a result of the continuing education of groups of Ethiopian civilians and soldiers alike. They felt increasingly that Ethiopia's modernization was proceeding too slowly under the existing regime, that high government officials were using their offices for personal aggrandizement, and that the Emperor bore primary responsibility for both of these and other ills of the country. From about 1955 on, the idea of overthrowing his regime attracted a number of these modernizing Ethiopians, some of whom formed small conspiratorial groups in which military and civilian circles were linked. By the end of the decade, a fairly large circle representing a number of the most able and progressive military and civilian leaders had agreed that forcible overthrow of Haile Selassie would be too disruptive, but that they would wait until he passed from the scene naturally to remove the objectionable hangers-on of his regime and take the reins of government into their own hands. A small segment of this circle, notably the Commander of the Imperial Bodyguard and his civilian brother, became too impatient to follow that policy and decided to carry out a coup d'état while the Emperor was out of the country on a state visit to Brazil. They were joined by the Chief of Security, who had himself been an officer of the Bodyguard previously. Their strategy was developed by a circle of about a dozen Bodyguard officers.[15]

Power was seized in the early hours of December 14, 1960, when after an initial roundup of the Crown Prince and other key dignitaries at the villa of the Empress, high government officials in Addis Ababa were summoned to Bodyguard Headquarters on the pretext that the Empress was seriously ill and were detained there under guard. Bodyguard soldiers seized control of communications and transportation lines, and established themselves at key points around Addis Ababa. The Chief of Police was quickly brought into the command circle, and the Police maintained order in the streets. At noon the titular head of the new government, the Crown Prince, read a message which proclaimed the end of "three thousand years" of oppression, ignorance, and poverty, and announced a policy of rapid modernization and political liberalization.

The Bodyguard leaders had instigated the coup on the blithe assumption that once the word was spoken, all patriotic forces would join hands to build the new society. They had underestimated the extent to which Army-Bodyguard tensions had been built up, the persisting adherence of the public to the old regime, and the degree to which Army commanders were disposed not to cooperate with the Bodyguard commander. Two key Army generals had escaped during the roundup of major political figures, however, and set up their own headquarters with the Army's First Division. Their group was joined by some highly influential civilians who had also eluded the rebels' net, notably the Vice-President of the Senate and the Patriarch of the Ethiopian Orthodox Church. The loyalist generals made contact with military commanders in provincial centers, mobilized additional troops and equipment from the provinces, and distributed counterrevolutionary leaflets to the populace of the capital. Negotiations between the two sides proved futile, and armed hostilities broke out on the afternoon of December 15. The Bodyguard forces were handicapped on several grounds: many of their troops were then stationed in the Congo; some officers deserted when it appeared that a bloodless coup was about to turn into civil war; some men deserted when they learned that they had been mobilized to overthrow the Emperor and not, as they had initially been told, to defend him; and their heaviest weaponry was light artillery. The Army had a potential of greatly superior numbers, as well as heavy artillery, a squadron of tanks, and the support of the air forces. The loyalist Army forces crushed the Bodyguard rebel forces after twenty-four hours of fighting, in which an estimated two thousand Ethiopians were killed or wounded. Meanwhile, the Emperor had flown back to Ethiopia, landing first in Asmara where his son-in-law, a brigadier-general, was provincial governor, and regained Addis Ababa on December 17.

1961–1966: Institutional Prominence and Political Involvement

The political position of the Army was decisively strengthened by its suppression of the attempted coup. Although the loyalist generals were subjected to virulent attacks in leaflets distributed by underground sympathizers with the coup, such dissidents were unable to sustain the momentum of the revolutionary moment. The Army emerged victorious over its old rival force, and self-important for having saved the Emperor's throne and demonstrating its vital role in preserving public order. Even many Ethiopians who shared the political aspirations of the leaders of the coup began to appreciate the prompt and resolute restoration, for it soon appeared quite certain that Army-Bodyguard solidarity in Addis Ababa would only have precipitated civil war on a national scale, since the Emperor would probably have reasserted his sovereignty through the forces commanded by his son-in-law in Eritrea.

Stimulated by this new prominence and sense of importance, the Armed Forces began to air grievances of their own which had long been suppressed. In the spring of 1961, in what was an unprecedented action, a large contingent of Army officers and men marched to the Palace and demanded a raise in pay. The Emperor had little choice but to acquiesce, and granted them what amounted to a budget increase of about Eth $2 million. About the same time, members of the Air Force went on strike for more pay. The Emperor tried to maintain control by assigning them to manual labor, but one group reportedly dug ditches at the Dire Dawa airport that hindered the traffic, and he was obliged to give them the salary increase after all.

The prominence of the Army has been strengthened by two other developments since 1960. Their participation in the United Nations military mission to the Congo, which involved a number of Army as well as Bodyguard men and officers, has brought them a good deal of prestige at home. Similarly, public appreciation of the military role has been enhanced by the security threat posed by Somali attacks and reprisals in the Ogaden. As a result, while military leaders may still be reluctant to seize control of the government while the Emperor remains in power, their political capability has been greatly increased.

CONCLUSIONS

THE TWO decades following Ethiopia's liberation witnessed a systematic, continuous build-up of the national military forces. One segment of those forces—the elite Imperial Bodyguard—became conspicuous for its special recruitment, training, esprit, experience, solidarity, and modernizing momentum. Observers at the end of the 1950's tended to see in the Bodyguard the most hopeful force for progressive national development. Established specifically to protect the Emperor against coup attempts, the Bodyguard seemed nevertheless a plausible agency for introducing and supporting a more aggressively efficient and modernizing regime. Bodyguard officers themselves began to feel increasingly a sense of political mission. The stage seemed set for the enactment of that stirring modern myth: a group of educated and devoted military men take over, sweep away a regime of corrupt and inefficient civilians, and shock a country into new spurts of nation building and social progress.

Ex post facto interpretations tend to see the defeat of the Bodyguard's attempt at a coup d'état as inevitable. Some of the participants themselves realized they had little chance, particularly after the first counter-revolutionary steps had been taken, but welcomed the chance to "speak the truth in the open" and set in motion the forces for more rapid change. They saw themselves as inaugurating a revolutionary tradition, much like the Russian officers of December, 1825, with whom they have often, and aptly, been compared.

While it is true that the actions of the Ethiopian Decembrists introduced some minor but significant changes in Ethiopia's political atmosphere, their experience has thrown some sobering light on the possible implications of military intervention in contemporary Ethiopia. Above all, the image of the military as a well-organized, highly unified force must be revised.

Rather than "rising as one man," as the Bodyguard officers idealistically expected, the Ethiopian military rose as twenty men, pursuing different lines of action for diverse ends. This is so for several reasons. First, as has been true throughout Ethiopian history, the military are not unified vis-à-vis civilian political leaders. High-ranking officers and civilian political leaders have much in common, are in close and frequent contact, and must be viewed ensemble as representing so many strands of individual interest and informal group affiliations. (This may well have the long-term beneficial effect of minimizing civilian-military tensions and enabling the military to feel that they can be effective and express their patriotic aspirations without having to be in complete control of the government.)

Second, the top military leaders live in a precarious network of communications among themselves, and the attempt at intervention is fraught with the danger of misunderstandings. Such misunderstandings are characteristic of Ethiopian political style, a style marked by considerable ambiguity and reserve, and apparently played a crucial part in polarizing the Commander of the Imperial Bodyguard and his chief antagonist, the Chief of Staff of the Armed Forces, who prior to the coup had been fairly close friends.

Third, the coup drew attention to the differing orientations of various groups within the military. The modernizing thrust of the younger trained officers was opposed by historically rooted forces in the military loyal to the old regime: the conservative sentiments and personal loyalties of some of the older or more senior officers, the traditionality of the lower ranks,[16] and the spirit of vast numbers of men in the provinces who would seize arms and rise in a moment for a chance to engage in some old-time manly warfare on behalf of King and Church.

The suppression of the December, 1960, coup by the Army has given its leaders an increased sense of power and responsibility for the continuity of Ethiopian politics, and impressed upon the public the importance of the Army in calculations about Ethiopia's political future. The stability of Haile Selassie's regime has been based on the overarching authority of a single man. When he goes, a condition of relative instability is likely to follow. Into that vacuum, ready or not, the military will be drawn. Since Ethiopia has not yet developed highly differentiated political institutions, a military take-over would not constitute the dismantling of democratic forms to the extent that it has in some other countries. Even so, many Ethiopians, including a number of military men, seem eager to push for more democratic institutions, and the traditional closeness of military and political functions in Ethiopia might mean that the military could make a considerable contribution without having actually to control the Government. With respect to the resources at their command, their value orientations and training, and the potential support of the public they are in a position to make a creditable contribution; but the disunity which continues to afflict them may limit their effectiveness for some time to come.

NOTES

1. The Amhara and the Tigreans are the two ethno-linguistic groups whose joint culture is sometimes referred to as "Abyssinian." The term "Abyssinia" will be used here in this technical sense when referring to Amhara-Tigre Society.

2. Ludolphus, Job, *A New History of Ethiopia.* Translated by J. P. Gent. 2d ed. London, 1684, p. 217.

3. Levine, Donald, "The Concept of Masculinity in Ethiopian Culture," *International Journal of Social Psychiatry,* vol. 12, 1966, pp. 17–23.

4. Such horizontal loyalties have, however, been of importance in the military organization of the Galla, whose traditional social organization is based on a system of age-graded classes.

5. Sambon, L., *L'esercito Abissino.* Rome, 1896, p. 9.

6. Levine, Donald, *Wax and Gold:* Tradition and Innovation in Ethiopian Culture. University of Chicago Press, Chicago, 1965, pp. 262–263, 272–273.

7. Perham, Margery, *The Government of Ethiopia.* Oxford University Press, New York, 1948, p. 167.

8. Pankhurst, Richard, "Fire-arms in Ethiopian History," *Ethiopia Observer,* vol. 6, no. 2, 1962.

9. Marcus, Harold, "Insurgency and Counter-insurgency in Ethiopia, 1936–1941." Unpublished manuscript, Department of History, Howard University.

10. Perham, Margery, *op. cit.,* pp. 200–206.

11. Kitchen, Helen, editor, *A Handbook of African Affairs.* Frederick A. Praeger, New York, 1964, pp. 197–198.

12. Levine, Donald, "Ethiopia: Identity, Authority and Realism," in Pye, Lucian W., and S. Verba, editors, *Political Culture and Political Development,* Princeton University Press, Princeton, N.J., 1965.

13. There may be certain regional exceptions to this generalization—the Tigreans in the region of Wajirat are said to have a much more cooperative and community orientation, for example—and it certainly does not apply to many of the ethnic groups outside the sphere of Amhara-Tigre culture. The generalization may also be qualified by noting the existence of a voluntary fraternal association, the *mahebar,* in Amhara-Tigre society,

an organization which has formed the model for a number of regional associations that have sprung up in Addis Ababa during the past decade.

14. Coward, H. R., *Military Technology in Developing Countries.* MIT Center for International Studies, Cambridge, Mass., 1964, p. 260.

15. See Greenfield, Richard, *Ethiopia: A New Political History,* Pall Mall Press, London, 1965, for a detailed account of the events of the coup.

16. Greenfield observes that "the influence of tradition on the lower ranks is very strong and it is a moot point as to whether the soldiers would remain loyal to the military High Command if its authority were challenged by a senior member of the aristocracy or by the Patriarch." *Ibid.,* p. 456.

Public Order and the Military in Africa:
Mutinies in Kenya, Uganda, and Tanganyika*
by Henry Bienen

THE overriding problems for most African countries are the maintenance of public order and the creation of political order.[1] The two
terms are not identical. "Public order" refers to a stable situation in
which the security of individuals or groups is not threatened and in
which disputes are settled without resort to violence. "Political order"
refers to a process of institution-building and the creation of stable patterns of politics. It is not some terminal state that exists forever, once
attained. Groups vie for authority and struggle for shares of valued
things, but they do so in a context of effective operation of political
instruments, through which both rulers and ruled act.[2] A crisis of
political order raises the specter of public disorder.

Problems of public disorder came most dramatically into focus as
violence broke out in the Congo after independence was granted in
1960. The Congo seemed to be an example of disorder that stemmed
from a failure of national integration in a country of great ethnic and
geographical diversities and in a context of precipitate withdrawal of
the colonial power.[3] Africa provides other examples of large-scale
turmoil which may have taken a greater toll of life and which were
marked by tribal or ethnic-religious violence; for example, the Sudan,
Nigeria, and Rwanda. The postcolonial history of most African countries, however, has not been marked by this kind of overt public disorder.

Perhaps because Africa has not been pervaded by violent public
disorder, the study of new African states has been organized in terms of

---

* On April 26, 1964, the Republic of Tanganyika merged with the
former sultanate of Zanzibar to form the United Republic of Tanzania. Because the Army mutiny occurred before the merger and is the main concern
of this case study, I refer throughout to Tanganyika rather than to Tanzania.

problems of development and integration. African elites have also discussed their problems in these terms. However, a concrete definition of problems of political development or national integration in Africa must account for a situation in which central or national authorities are unable to exert authority over the territorial entity they "rule." This phenomenon is not unique to Africa. The claims of any central government to rule must be measured against the realities of local autonomy, de jure or de facto. Many areas of life in which centralized determination is taken for granted in western polities which call themselves "decentralized," "loose," or "democratic" are outside the scope or even the reach of national authorities in Africa. In the power realm, nationwide political structures are either nonexistent or too weak to enforce the will of ruling national elites, no matter whether they are of traditional lineage groups, civilian bureaucracy, or the military. There is a failure of centralized authority in the realm of legitimacy. Although many African one-party states claim that only disciplined parties can mobilize for development, it is often in these very states that values are not authoritatively allocated for the society as a whole by central authorities.[4]

Highly localized determination of political life need not be synonymous with disorder, anarchy, and chaos. In fact, it may be the only way to avoid these conditions in certain circumstances. A problem of political order arises when some national or central body tries to bring its rule over subnational entities. Whether a problem of public order develops depends on the nature of the resistance to this effort. Similarly, subnational groups, political organizations, or governments may struggle with each other for control of the center or for other reasons. The form and substance of the struggle determine whether a crisis of political order exists. Thus, to make a judgment about the kind of order problem that exists when some local unit cannot enforce compliance within its own boundaries, we should know what kind of effort is being resisted, how the resistance is being manifested, and what the governing body is doing to secure compliance. Usually, it is not difficult to make such a determination. For African countries, public disorder is a constant threat because political order is fragile or has not even been achieved.

Africa has many political, economic, and social incongruities because certain patterns of actions are national in scope, while others, parallel or intersecting, are not. For example, many African countries have communication systems which now provide rather easy dissemination of ideas and mobility within national boundaries. A monetary sector of the economy may co-exist spatially with a subsistence sector in every region, tribal area, and natural geographic unit; but individuals who live near each other in terms of miles can live worlds apart if one grows cash crops, and another does not. National institutions—armies, parliaments, heads of states, political parties—have a presence and a real meaning, but they may not be able to enforce their orders throughout most of the country and may be ignored in various degrees by the majority of the people. One of the most striking incongruities is the existence of elites who strive to rule their countries from capitals or regional centers but who cannot impose their wishes on local elites and who reach nonelites little, if at all. We may feel that anarchy exists because national elites are in fact trying to make their will felt. We then speak of a collapse or breakdown of order when we really mean the failure of central rule.[5]

The problem of public order has been posed in another connection in Africa. In 1965–1966 civilian authority failed dramatically as the military seized power in Congo-Kinshasa, Dahomey, Central African Republic, Upper Volta, Nigeria, and Ghana. Army leaders who took power did so in the name of averting disorder. In Nigeria, Congo, and Upper Volta, disorder actually existed, but there were no indications that this situation was about to occur in Ghana. In Nigeria, the Army was itself responsible for furthering breakdowns of public order, as in East Africa in 1964 when the Armies of Kenya, Uganda, and Tanganyika had themselves disrupted public order.

In Africa the claim has also been made that military elites are suited for short-term clean-up of corruption, for starting or revitalizing economic development, and for preserving or establishing national integration because the military speaks for the entire nation, without regard to religious or parochial tribal distinctions. Almost everywhere the short-term aspects of military rule are stressed. The norms of a civilian-ruled polity seem to be accepted, so far, by the military in Africa. At least Army leaders speak of a return to civilian rule.[6]

The reasons military elites are able successfully to intervene and are motivated to do so are obvious. In a situation in which all institutions operate from weakness, if the military exists at all, it is an important political organization. No matter the degree of professionalization within the officer corps, the level of technology, the organizational format of a particular military force, an army/police in Africa is always a potential political factor because it can exert some strength in what is essentially a domestic power vacuum. Moreover, the military *claims* to be a national group rather than a parochial one; and if the claim is widely accepted, the military then constitutes a reservoir of legitimate authority. We cannot take for granted this reservoir of authority.[7] Not every military elite thinks of itself as reflecting and incorporating national aspirations, although this may be an area where "demonstration effects" are at work and the military in one country begins to conceive of itself in this way after contact with other militaries or after seeing military take-overs made in these terms. Even when the military considers itself the embodiment of national ideals, the population at large may not accept this claim. When the military enters the political arena as a ruling group, the reservoir, if one has existed, has a tendency to run dry quite quickly. Nonetheless, when civilian governments are discredited, the military may be able to intervene without force because it does retain legitimacy untainted by civilian failures.

Of course, the technology of the military in new states is relevant for intervention in domestic politics. "The military" usually means infantry battalions which can be deployed in urban centers. These battalions are sometimes supplemented by airborne troops and a special forces police which may have some motorized weaponry. Army and police are often both national forces and constitute a kind of super-police.[8] (As armies grow and the military comes to include artillery and airborne units, greater distinction between police and army is likely.)

We cannot generalize easily about the ideology of military leaders, because both the social origins of officers and their career lines differ within and between African countries. We can, however, say that military leaders are peculiarly indisposed to tolerate public disorder—even if their actions sometimes lead to such a state. There are less certain grounds to argue that they are also indisposed to tolerate corruption, lack of economic development, tribalism, or parochialism of any kind. Military leaders have been accused of and implicated in corrupt activities.[9] They have been deeply involved in the very systems they overthrew in Ghana and Nigeria. And the military itself is often driven by ethnic cleavages and it acts as an interest group at times not even pretending to be acting in the national interest but rather making overt interest group demands. The East African mutinies of 1964 were a case in point. While the military may be indisposed to disorder, it may be the prime mover for disorder. The instruments of violence are not always used in the interest of stability. The Force Publique's mutiny in the Congo was, after all, not only a response to a breakdown of authority but also a cause of chaos. The mutinous Armies in Tanganyika, Uganda, and Kenya tried to take advantage of governmental weakness to put forward their demands and in so doing created disorder. In Tanganyika this led to riots by elements of the population of Dar es Salaam. President Olympio was assassinated by soldiers in Togo in circumstances that remain as yet unclear.

It remains to be seen whether the military leaders who took power in 1965–1966 will be able to solve economic and political problems. Already it is being maintained that the military can be more effective than a political party and that this is one of the most significant factors in the changed African scene since 1964.[10] But there is some doubt already that the Army and police are stable and powerful factors in otherwise fluid and powerless societies.[11] Stable they are not. Their societies are fluid and often no groups are able to impose some central rule over the whole society. But this does not mean that African societies have no power groups or that the military will be able to remake societies in their own image, provided they have one.

Since the military has intervened so widely in Africa, and probably will continue to do so, it is essential to detail the nature of the interaction of the military with its environment. To determine the situation in a specific country, it is important to know the composition of the military elite and the structure and size of the total military force. More generally, it is important to consider how the military fits into the political system and what social and economic constraints, as well as political ones, are imposed on the form and substance of military intervention.

I have chosen to examine the East African mutinies of January, 1964, in order to approach the questions of public order and nature of military intervention in Africa. The mutinies of the two infantry battalions of the Tanganyika Rifles and elements of the Uganda Rifles and Kenya Rifles demonstrated clearly the relationship between the military and civilian authorities in Africa and the problem of creating authoritative structures, although the Armies were not trying to and never seized power. In fact, the very parochialness of the Armies' demands and the vulnerability of ostensibly popular civilian governments were illustrated. Moreover, the nature of the military force itself was revealed, with regard to its internal composition, organization, and leadership, as well as its relationship to the police and to interest groups.[12]

The three East African Armies never did assume power. In East Africa it would not have been difficult to topple governments. To constitute a military government would be another matter. This situation never occurred because British troops intervened to uphold constituted rule in Kenya, Uganda, and Tanganyika. The British intervention is important because non-African states have influenced the nature of the military in Africa (although not always its role), through their provision of equipment, training, organization, and an ethos for African military forces. And great powers overtly have been the final arbiters of military intervention in the Congo (Brazzaville and Leopoldville), the three East African cases, and Gabon.

THE MILITARY IN EAST AFRICA

A GREAT deal of the literature about the military in new states has dealt with elites. Edward Shils, for example, discussed the military, stressing officer classes, the intelligentsia, gaps between towns and countryside, and disparities in education and socialization among segments of a population. Shils' category of modernizing military oligarchies described a system where a military elite constitutes itself as a ruling group. However, he noted that most African countries have no indigenous military elite.[13] This is less true today than it was at the start of the 1960's; Africanization of officer corps has taken place. Still, African armies are small in terms of absolute size and as a percentage of the total population. Many officers are either recently graduated from a short course in military affairs abroad or, more rarely, from military institutes where they matriculated. Some are former noncommissioned officers from World War II promoted during the current Africanization program.[14] With this in mind, we must immediately consider the term "military rule" itself. Generals or colonels may sieze power and claim to be ruling a nation in the name of the Army, but no "modern" military elite exists in any Sub-Saharan African country because the number of officers is so small and African officers with western officer training are so recent.[15]

At the time of the mutinies in January, 1964, the East African military forces were examples of African armies which were essentially battalions officered by expatriates.[16] Kenya's officer corps was more Africanized at the time of independence (December, 1963) than either the Tanganyika Army at the time of independence (December, 1961) or the Uganda Army at independence (October, 1962).[17] But the three Armies were very similar because they were all formed from the British-trained and -commanded King's African Rifles; in addition, they all had little firepower and no tanks or artillery. The Kenya Army had more mobility and firepower than the others, since it possessed scout cars, more troop carriers, and light mortars. Kenya's advantage in weaponry and transport stemmed from its needs in its northern territories, where it was and still is confronted with Somalia's territorial demands and the hostile activities of Somali *shiftas* or guerrillas. Furthermore, Kenya was a main British base in Africa, and the British had put more hardware into Kenya than into Uganda and Tanganyika. And finally, the Kenya police force was by far the largest and best equipped in East Africa, since it had been developed during the Mau Mau crisis of the 1950's. At the end of 1963, Kenya had three Army battalions of 2,500 men and a 11,500-man police force. Uganda had one battalion until 1963, when another was added, bringing the Army near to 2,000 men. The Uganda police force was 5,500, not including the separate police force of the Kingdom of Buganda, which totaled around 600, although there were close to 200 Buganda in the Uganda police.[18] Tanganyika's Army and police force were slightly smaller than Uganda's, although even before the January, 1964, mutiny the government was thinking about increasing the size of the Army and establishing an Air Force.

The United Kingdom and Israel were providing Tanganyika and Uganda with military assistance, and Britain was both assisting Kenya's military force and defraying items in the defense budget. The stated annual defense budgets were under $1.75 million each for all three countries, and none of them wanted to increase defense expenditures. Africanization of the officer corps had proceeded slowly, precisely because East African political leaders were trying to keep costs down. Officers were paid very well by local standards. Any expansion in numbers of officers or replacement of British was bound to push up defense costs. Enlisted men were perhaps less realistically treated. They were not paid particularly well compared to semiskilled wage labor in the civilian economy. Furthermore, enlisted men and noncommissioned officers did exist in larger numbers than officers and could act as a pressure group. After independence, their grievances over wages were at the root of the mutinies. Political leaders had not appreciated the depth of discontent in the Armies.

It is often argued that African countries cannot afford and do not need Armies because their security problems are internal. In any case, no African country could withstand aggression from a major non-African power. Furthermore, it is claimed that African resolution to settle disputes without force, pan-Africanism, and the Organization of African Unity (OAU) are going to obviate the necessity of Armies. African political leaders have sometimes sounded these very themes. Many have been sorrowful about the creation and expansion of their Armies. When he was Prime Minister, President Nyerere of Tanganyika said, "We'd rather spend our money on bread [than on an Army]."[19] Yet many African countries do have external security problems, which are particularly severe in East Africa.

Kenya continues to face demands made on its northern territories by Somalia and the Kenya police and Army have been engaged in countering Somali raiders who live within and without Kenya. The border between Tanganyika and Kenya has not always been quiet as tribes move across it in their migratory patterns.[20] Tanganyika has had disturbances on almost all its borders. Its long Lake Tanganyika border with the Congo was the pathway for various Congolese factions to cross into Tanganyika. And Tanganyika played an important role in supplying eastern Congolese opponents of the Congo Central Government through Kigoma, the major Tanganyika town on the lake. Rwanda has been unstable since its own independence in 1962. Rwandan refugees came into northwestern Tanganyika during 1962–1963 and the border has been highly unstable. Tanganyika has had hostile relations with Malawi on one part of its southern border. And even its border with Zambia was disturbed during the Lumpa uprising in Zambia. Above all, Tanganyika has been a major base for liberation movements in southern Africa and has been a sanctuary and staging ground for Mozambique freedom fighters. Tanganyika Army units have faced on Mozambique. The movement of refugees and guerrillas into Tanganyika has created internal as well as external security problems as men with arms and families without means of sustenance move into the territory.[21]

Uganda, too, has had extremely tense border situations and very pronounced internal security problems. It shares a long land border with the Congo and faces on the area which saw the most intense fighting in the Congo during 1963–1965. Sudanese refugees coming down from the north and Rwandans coming up from the south have created problems. Nomadic tribes have raided Uganda territory from Kenya, an example of what has been called "war subsystems,"[22] that is, the feuding of pastoral tribes and clans. This feuding is pronounced among the northeastern Uganda nomadic tribes, the Karamojong and the Turkana. Uganda also has its "rejection movements," that is, movements which either want complete separatism from Uganda, some form of autonomy, or separation from some particular Kingdom or district administrator. The Ruwenzururu movement of western Uganda, the struggle between Sebei and Bagisu around Mt. Elgon, the lost countries issue between Buganda and Bunyoro, and the place of Buganda within Uganda are all examples. Uganda, which has by far the highest murder rate in East Africa (one murder for about every 10,000 people) also suffers from organized gang violence, called *kondoism*.[23] In a country which has one policeman for every 1,000 people, of whom only one in ten lives in a town, relatively wealthy cash crop farmers who live rather far apart provide a target for organized gangs. Thus, about 14 per cent of recurrent expenditures is devoted to police and prisons alone. Part of the Army expenditure is devoted to internal security as well, since the Army has policed, albeit ineffectively, the Western Kingdom of Toro where the Ruwenzururu movement is located.

The small Armies of East Africa might be thought to have enough to do policing borders and carrying out internal security functions; but in these countries as elsewhere in Africa, there has been a feeling that Armies ought to perform constructive social and economic work.

The French made nonmilitary use of Armies before they granted independence, and some independent French-speaking states continued to use the Army for compulsory agricultural work and for road building. The role of the Army as a modernizing and integrating force in society has sometimes been stressed. The Israeli model is cited by African politicians, who claim that men from all areas and tribes will "melt" in the Army and that they will bridge gaps between the state and society. The Army will, they say, stand as a symbol of the nation while it performs real nation-building tasks.

Within East Africa, such ideas were most explicitly stated in Tanganyika. When Oscar Kambona was Minister for External Affairs and Defense, his speeches stressed the importance of the Army for economic development and national integration. President Nyerere has always talked about the Army as an instrument for nation-building. In Kenya and Uganda, political leaders spoke publicly in a similar vein, but little was done to employ the military in economic or social service projects. Army personnel did clear land on training assignments, but they were much more likely to appear for ceremonial occasions than as part of a systematic program for development. Furthermore, despite pressure from the youth wings of ruling political parties, particularly the Tanganyika Youth League of the Tanganyika African National Union (TANU)[24] and Uganda People's Congress (UPC) youth group, and despite the inclinations of some political leaders to use the youth wings as a military or paramilitary force, recruitment procedures for the Army remained the same as the preindependent selection process. In Uganda, the recruitment bias for northerners was retained since the political leadership of the UPC was itself northern-based. But the men recruited were not necessarily political followers or even politically aware. Rather, they were picked for the martial virtues: physical fitness, combativeness, and so on. In Tanganyika, recruiting teams traveled about, signing up men with the same characteristics. The choices often were made by noncommissioned officers who had themselves been professional soldiers in the King's African Rifles. In 1963, the two tribes that had traditionally supplied many Army recruits—the Hehe of central Tanganyika and the Kuria of the Lake Victoria littoral —were reported to be still supplying 25 per cent each of new recruits.[25] Training courses remained British-oriented and lacked education content.[26] And although the government announced its intention to have universal male registration for military and nation-building purposes, no universal military training or conscription program was implemented.

In Kenya, the Army mutiny broke out less than a month after independence. The internal self-government of the ruling Kenya African National Union (KANU) regime itself was only seven months old.[27] Yet the KANU government had begun to inject a new note into recruitment and organization of Army and police forces. In Kenya, the opposition Kenya African Democratic Union (KADU), which drew its strength from tribal groups outside Kikuyu, Luo, and Kamba (the three largest in Kenya), had argued for localization of police power in line with its determination to maintain strong regional and subregional political and administrative entities. When the *Majimbo* Constitution, which had defined a Kenya of strong regions was abolished after the KANU victory, police powers became increasingly centralized in fact as well as in theory. But at the same time, within the ruling KANU party, individual leaders struggled to see Kamba, Luo, or Kikuyu in responsible police and Army positions and the Luo-Kikuyu leadership of KANU began to try to end the dominance of Kamba within the Army.[28] At the same time, Luo-Kikuyu rivalry for patronage posts in the military and positions of influence proceeded and remains still. This, however, was not a result of the infusion of military and police into the politics of nation-building or modernization but of a struggle for power defined in tribal-political terms long familiar in Kenya.

Because of this struggle, Kenya's political leadership more self-consciously attempted to master its own military force. This attempt was obscured because Kenya came to independence later than Uganda and Tanganyika and because the British retained a much greater military presence in Kenya through bases and training programs. In Tanganyika, the government believed itself popular—and with real justification. TANU had won overwhelming electoral victories, and Nyerere was liked throughout the country. Government and TANU leaders took for granted Army loyalty and treated the Army as another institution they had inherited from the British colonial regime. There had never been a struggle between civil servants and political leaders in Tanganyika. The idea of nation-building, as expressed by Nyerere and top TANU leaders (but not all middle-level leaders in TANU), conceived of a unity by amalgamation; there was no feeling that the civil service or military had to be radically remodeled right away or purged. The aim was to create a synthesis of state and party institutions over time.[29] And for the immediate future, the TANU government saw advantages to preserving civil service and Army as political institutions.

In Uganda, the UPC leadership and particularly the inside group around Prime Minister Obote had close ties with the few Uganda officers who were also northerners. The main political problems for the UPC were the place of Buganda and politically organized Catholicism, which was the base for the Democratic Party. UPC leaders felt secure about the Army of northerners on both these issues.

Specific political issues were largely irrelevant to the causes and outcomes of the East African mutinies. All three governments were fragile in terms of the overriding internal problems they faced. But the decisive factor was the fragility of ruling institutions in East Africa per se. Although one could argue that by the end of 1963 Uganda, Tanganyika, and Kenya were in different phases in their respective political dynamics and that their internal problems had important differences, it was the striking similarities of the inability of the governments to deal with essentially parochial demands of enlisted men and noncommissioned officers which revealed the crisis of order in East Africa and which is illustrative for Africa as a whole.[30] The time factor was of importance, not as much in comparing the three East African situations but in comparing East Africa and West Africa. The absence of an East African officer corps distinguished the East African Armies from Ghanaian and Nigerian Armies which had been Africanizing their officers over a ten-year period or from the former French territories, which underwent a crash Africanization program in their Armies from 1956–1960.[31] Thus, there were no East African officers who could, by virtue of rank and authority, control or head off mutinous enlisted men. On the other hand, the absence of a corporate officer group inhibited the transformation of a strike for more pay into an overt demand for military control of government or military participation in civilian regimes. The lack of indigenous officers was a mixed blessing.

THE MUTINIES

LATE on Sunday night, January 19, 1964, troops of the first battalion in Dar es Salaam left the Colito Barracks located some eight miles from the center of the city. They came into Dar es Salaam and quickly took control of key points: radio station, police stations, airport, and State House—the home and office of President Nyerere.[32] During the early morning hours the mutinous troops, led by a sergeant, rounded up British officers who lived in a residential area between the barracks and the city. They had already seized the British officers at the barracks, although the Tanganyika Rifles' Commander, Brigadier Patrick Sholto Douglas, escaped. The leader of the mutiny, Sergeant Ilogi, offered the command of the Army to Lieutenant Elisha Kavona, the only university graduate among the Tanganyika officers. He had not been in on the plot but "thought it prudent to accept."[33]

At first, the mutineers made only two demands. They wanted to get rid of their thirty-five British officers and they wanted higher pay.[34] The mutineers negotiated with Ministers, for both the President and Vice-President Kawawa were in hiding. Oscar Kambona, the Minister for External Affairs and Defense, who was also Secretary General of TANU, was the major governmental negotiator. He was unable to end the mutiny although he succeeded in limiting demands so that no overtly political ones were made.

During these first two days, the police remained on the sidelines.[35] The police force had lost its field force, that is, its best armed and most martial troops, because 300 of them had been shipped to Zanzibar after the Zanzibar Revolution. The Dar es Salaam Army battalion met no resistance of any kind. Apparently, the Minister for Home Internal Affairs requested Kenya troops but the Minister for External Affairs later countermanded this order, probably doubting their reliability.[36] The 800-man second battalion of Tanganyika Rifles at Tabora, which is about 400 miles northwest of Dar es Salaam, mutinied on January 21. They seized their British officers and their senior African officer, Captain M. S. H. Sarakikya, who is now the ranking Tanzanian officer and a brigadier.[37] The Tabora mutiny led to early and limited looting; but once Sarakikya gained control, the looting stopped.

In Dar es Salaam, however, looting was more severe. The breakdown in public order, the absence of Nyerere, the incapacity of his ministers to end the mutiny, the careful and quiet action or nonaction of the police, all created a situation in which mobs formed easily. Hostility to Asians and Arabs was expressed and interracial killing broke out in some quarters of the city. Initially, some soldiers looted, but later the Army moved to control looting.

President Nyerere emerged on January 21, and the leaders of the mutiny reiterated that they wanted no coup, only Africanization and higher wages. Neither the President nor Mr. Kambona was able to get the troops back to their barracks. The President tried to minimize what had occurred. He never defined "the trouble" as a mutiny, although he made it clear that he believed the whole affair was a disgrace and had done irreparable damage to Tanganyika. In his broadcasts to the people he seemed still under the constraint of the mutineers.[38] And in fact, it was not until British troops landed on January 25 from HMS Centaur, which had been lying off the Tanganyika coast, and took Colito Barracks, scattering the first battalion into the bush with some little loss of life, that the Mutiny can be said to have come to an end.[39]

Between January 21 and 25, the mutiny began to take on more political tones. No revolt of military force could be without major political implications. But it was only after the mutiny had started that dissi-

dent trade-union leaders, political opponents of TANU, and a handful
of dissidents within TANU emerged to take advantage of the situation
and to make explicit political demands. Political demands were not expressed during the Kenya and Uganda mutinies simply because the
mutinies did not last as long there and because government leaders,
less caught by surprise, were able to take stronger stands.

Logistical factors rather than a disparate political context led to a
different pattern in Kenya and Uganda from that of Tanganyika. Just
as the mutiny spread from Dar es Salaam to Tabora, it spread from
Tanganyika to Uganda and Kenya. The demands in the latter two countries were the same: Africanization of the Army and higher pay for enlisted men and noncommissioned officers. The physical contiguity of
the three countries, the basic similarity in internal Army organization,
and relationship of the Army to British officers and training programs;
and the analogous place of Army to society in general and political
leadership in particular made likely the rapid infection of mutiny from
one country to the other. No *explicandum* of foreign subversion is necessary.[40] Nor were common East African military arrangements per se
responsible for the contagion. There were no such arrangements by
1964.[41]

There was, however, a signal event in the political history of East
Africa which formed the backdrop to the mutinies and helps to explain
why the first link in the chain was Tanganyika. On January 12, 1964,
the government of the Sultan of Zanzibar, which had only recently been
installed, was overthrown.[42] Never before in East Africa had an independent government been confronted with force in the name of revolutionary government. Never since the British overthrew indigenous
rulers and drove the Germans out of East Africa had force been successful in replacing one government with another. Of all the East African countries, Tanganyika had been characterized, prior to 1964, as the
one where violence as a means of obtaining change had been virtually
nonexistent. True, during the German colonial period, the Hehe of the
southern highlands had fought against the colonial rulers in the 1890's;
and again southern tribes fought against the Germans in the widespread
Maji-Maji Revolt of 1905–1907. These were the most widespread and
intense struggles against colonial rule in East Africa until the outbreak
of Mau-Mau in Kenya. But since 1907, aside from the British fight
against the Germans in World War I in Tanganyika, there had been

neither revolt nor the large-scale tribal violence which characterized Uganda's separatist movements.

Thus, violence and the overthrow of constituted rule in Zanzibar made an immediate and deep impact in Tanganyika. This impact was even greater because the Sultan's rule was ended not only in the name of African nationalism against a minority Arab rule supported by foreign imperialists, but it was also made in the name of a class war of workers and peasants against exploiters. The shock waves from Zanzibar traveled rapidly across the narrow sea to Tanganyika. Legitimacy had been called into question. Dissident groups were more willing to use illegitimate means in the three East African countries than they had been before the Zanzibar Revolution. Tanganyika, the closest to Zanzibar geographically, and with the most intimate political connections, felt the first and deepest impact.

Another event triggered the Dar es Salaam mutiny. Two weeks before its outbreak, President Nyerere made a major policy speech. On January 7, he asserted that preference would no longer be given to Africans over other citizens of Tanganyika. Formerly, the policy had been one of localization but with an emphasis on redressing the imbalance in the number of Africans who held responsible posts. Now Nyerere linked a policy of no discrimination against Tanganyika citizens to the needs of a new Five Year Plan which would require utilizing all the trained personnel available. This speech alarmed trade-union officials, including the assistant general secretary of the Kenya Federation of Labour, who feared that Tanganyika had dropped its policy of Africanization.[43] The Army was disturbed too, although the speech did not affect the Army because all officers were British expatriates and not non-African Tanganyika citizens.[44] Nor were there non-African noncommissioned officers or enlisted men. In fact, according to one reporter, senior British officers and the Ministry of Defense "were already working out, on the initiative of British officers, a plan for the complete Africanization of the officer corps by the end of 1964."[45]

At the very start of the Tanganyika mutiny, the Ugandan government showed its sensitivity to the question of Africanization when the Minister of the Interior, Felix Onama, expressed confidence in British officers but announced plans to bring companies under African command by the end of 1964 and battalions by the end of 1965.[46] Despite Mr. Onama's remarks of January 22, elements of the Uganda battalion stationed at Jinja mutinied on January 23. Jinja is about 50 miles east of Kampala, Uganda's major town and capital and a little farther yet from Entebbe, the administrative headquarters. Jinja was the main Army base although many troops were at several points on the Rwanda, Congo, and Sudan borders. Others were in the Kingdom of Toro, trying without effect to end the Ruwenzururu rebellion; troops were also at Moroto in the far north of Uganda near Kenya. Prime Minister Obote justified his appeal for British troops on the grounds that security forces were stretched thin across Uganda and "unruly elements," which existed in all countries, might try to take advantage of this situation. No doubt he had the riots in Dar es Salaam very much in mind in the context of Uganda's own explosive town population and tribal, regional, and religious difficulties. At the same time that he called on British troops (they came from Kenya and from British ships off the East African coast), Mr. Obote promised an upward revision of pay, said British troops would not be needed long, and called the mutiny a "sit-down strike," denying a mutiny had occurred and affirming the loyalty of the troops. Indeed, the mutinous troops had held Mr. Onama prisoner for a while but they never left Jinja to head toward Kampala. The difference between being eight miles away and more than fifty miles proved important. The troops could not have had the element of surprise they achieved in Dar es Salaam. A small number of police might have held them up on the Kampala-Jinja road. And because of the dispersion of the Uganda Army throughout the country, there was no large concentration of troops in any one spot. Political leaders might find a number of morals here based on geography and the advantages of stationing armies away from capitals.

Kenya's political leaders received these blessings, too. Furthermore, British troops were already on Kenya soil and could be called on immediately. On January 24, Prime Minister Kenyatta moved to head off a Kenya mutiny. He announced a plan to increase the size of the Kenya Rifles by 1,000; he admitted that there were certain "anomalies" in the pay of African soldiers. And at the same time, British troops were on the move in Kenya and coming into Kenya from Aden. Nonetheless, two barracks mutinies occurred that night. One was at Langata Barracks a few miles outside Nairobi, Kenya's capital, and the other was at Lanet Barracks near Nakuru about one hundred miles northwest of Nairobi along the main Uganda-Kenya road. In Nairobi the British quickly seized control of key points and in Nakuru they took the armory. At Nakuru African officers and sergeants as well as at least 150 soldiers remained loyal. By January 25, the Kenya mutiny had ended. On this same day the British moved to end Tanganyika's unsettled situation by disarming the troops there. And in Uganda, British soldiers surrounded the camp at Jinja, seized the armory, and induced the mutineers to surrender.

The repercussions for the three countries seemed to vary in severity in accordance with the degree of length and disruptiveness of the mutiny. President Nyerere had the worst situation. He had called in the British after losing control. Furthermore, the Tanganyika Army was in ruins. Many mutinous troops were put in detention and tried. Others were sent back to their homes. The two battalions of the Tanganyika Rifles were disbanded, and it was determined to build an entirely new Army. Meanwhile, Nigerian troops were requested to provide security after the British left and until new battalions could be formed. Demonstrations were held in support of the President in Dar es Salaam and district and regional centers. It was reported that when Nyerere said he was sorry to have called in British troops, there were chants of "We forgive you."[47]

THE MUTINIES RECONSIDERED

THE collapse of government authority in Tanganyika and the reliance on British troops in Uganda and Kenya made it abundantly clear that whatever the popularity of the governments involved and the personal position of individual leaders, the East African governments could neither prevent mutinies nor counter them once they occurred. However, although the mutineers could have brought down the government in Dar es Salaam had they wished, and but for the presence of British troops they could have done it in Uganda and Kenya, too, the Armies could not necessarily have replaced the civilian governments.

In Tanganyika, it would be one thing to occupy the capital and another to impose rule over the whole country—to command the regional and district political and administrative hierarchies. The Army had neither the personnel nor the will to do so. Nor could the Army take for granted even the support that TANU gets as the party which brought the country to independence. One does not have to argue that TANU "mobilizes" the population through a network of functioning party organizations in order to affirm that the party does legitimate the orders that civil servants give and does provide self-legitimation and authority for political leaders who form the government. The Army had no place in the popular consciousness throughout the country so that it could compete with TANU as a legitimizing force. It provided no symbol of the nation as a whole; it was not seen as an organization which stood above politics and self-interest.

Even where political opposition to the ruling party was overt and organized as in Kenya and Uganda, the Armies did not provide any possible alternative to civilian rule. In Uganda, the Army would have been seen as even more "northern" and non-Bantu than the ruling UPC. Because of its ethnic composition, the Army would have faced even more severe integrative problems than the UPC. In Kenya the Army with its Kamba dominance would have faced similar Kikuyu and Luo opposition. Armies in new states are particularly vulnerable to problems stemming from ethnic and religious heterogenity, because the Army is itself often associated with specific ethnic groups and because the norms of the military may lead to an insensitivity to ethnic-religious values. And these are not mutually exclusive possibilities.

Army personnel sent to administer or to oversee politically districts in any of the East African countries would have been even more cut off from the local population than the political leaders and civil servants on the spot. We have seen how necessary is the collaboration of civil servants to new military rulers in Ghana, Nigeria, the Sudan, and elsewhere. In East Africa, there had been some hostility between civil servants and political leaders. The civil servants considered the political leaders less educated and less knowledgeable, and the politicians sometimes resented civil service lack of support for the national movement before independence and condescending attitudes after it. But in Tanganyika, in particular, where Africanization of the civil service came late, where there are many contacts between civil servants and politicians, and where Nyerere always emphasized a community between them, politician antagonisms were never very far-reaching. And this was true in East Africa as a whole compared to states in West Africa— Nigeria, Ivory Coast, and Ghana in particular (where there were more developed and entrenched civil service) or compared to Mali and Guinea (where civil servants may feel themselves under political pressure). In some African countries civil servants may feel themselves more radical than the political leaders; in others, a more radically sounding political leadership stands out. In East Africa, civil servants have had no political stance per se. But they undoubtedly would have found one in an Army-run regime which came into existence through a coup. For the civil servants would have felt freer to make interest group demands; they would have felt their compliance essential to maintenance of the regime; and they would have felt themselves vastly better educated than privates and noncommissioned officers, who had little formal education.

Furthermore, whether civil servants in East Africa are technical specialists or administrative generalists, they rely on district and regional party officials to put their programs into effect. Where bureaucratic norms are not widely understood or accepted and where outsiders have a difficult time exerting their influence, it is hard to see how Army men posted to a district could in fact get compliance, given the small coercionary apparatus at their disposal.

It would be tempting to conclude that at least at the center government must have been indeed fragile in Tanganyika since a battalion of a thousand men could control the command points without opposition from either the body politic or any organized group. But would this be an accurate assessment? The mutineers had an advantage, because Dar es Salaam is cut off from the rest of Tanganyika's population centers. It would have been difficult to mobilize people from outside the capital to move against the Army (just as the Army could not easily have forayed out into the countryside). During the mutinies the regional and district headquarters, with the exception of Tabora and Nachingwea, continued to be run by the TANU and civil service hierarchies. There was apprehension in places but no looting in the towns or countryside. In some districts, instability at the center led to attempts to settle old scores, but only rarely did people try to get rid of local TANU leaders. When it was clear that order was reestablished in Dar es Salaam, some local TANU leaders did try to imprison those who had openly opposed them. But on the whole, the regions and districts stayed calm, probably because of their removal from the center, the difficulty in communications, and the diffuseness of local politics. These conditions themselves have made it difficult, if not impossible, for the Army to impose itself over the sixty districts which comprise the seventeen regions of Tanganyika.

The Army would have faced all the problems that the present TANU leaders face, many of which confront most African leaders: a sparsely settled country with its population in major clusters along the peripheries; an economy which does not provide the material requisites for exerting central control; regional, district, and village organizations which operate with a great deal of autonomy; severe personnel shortages; the persistence of traditional patterns of social, political, and economic behaviors. Furthermore, the mutineers would be dislodging the figure with the greatest popularity and authority in Tanganyika—Julius Nyerere. An army without trained administrators would have had to rule without the center that did exist—those few national leaders who have the consent of their party and civil service hierarchies to rule even if they cannot exert close control over those hierarchies.

Since the Army did not claim to be ruling, a wait-and-see attitude prevailed even among TANU activists within Dar es Salaam. Naturally, there was a disinclination for unarmed men to oppose armed soldiers. What is striking in retrospect is that so few people took advantage of a chaotic situation to push their own ambitions. At the top, the President and at least one of the ministers[48] called attention to the loyalty of the Minister for Defense, Oscar Kambona, who negotiated with the rebels when the President went underground. Kambona had been accused within Tanganyika and in the West of being ambitious and radical. When the President praised Kambona's courage in reducing the effects of the troops' mutiny, he was doing more than voicing his appreciation; he was asserting that TANU had stayed united.[49]

Since TANU Annual Conference and National Executive Committee meetings were due to convene just as the mutiny broke out, there was ample opportunity for TANU regional and district leaders to take part in any revolt along with middle-level leaders or dissident top leaders who resided in Dar es Salaam. Of the more than 200 regional and district leaders who came into Dar es Salaam, only one—a Tanu district secretary and head of government in the district (area commissioner) —was implicated. No parliamentary secretary (junior minister) was involved. Certain chiefs and Muslim leaders (sometimes the same people) who had opposed TANU, or as in the case of the leading dissident, Chief Fundikira, a former TANU Minister who had broken with the party, were not connected with the mutiny.[50] No civil servants were involved.

There were very good reasons for the solid loyalty from civil servants and from middle-level TANU leaders. Aside from Nyerere's personal popularity and the cohesiveness of his ministers and their personal loyalty to him, the dangers of trying to make common cause with the mutineers should have been apparent to any would-be leader of a coup. The soldiers did not distinguish between shades of political opinion within the Cabinet or within TANU. When they were in the streets they were as likely to attack a parliamentary secretary who had taken a radical position on economic policy or even on Africanization as one who had not. Any government official was an "in"; the mutineers saw themselves as "outs." They wanted a bigger slice of the pie. Only some disaffected trade-union leaders, whose demands for higher pay and Africanization were the same as the soldiers' demands and who knew the trade unions would be governmentalized in any case, joined in. Most of the leadership of the Tanganyika Federation of Labour did not—for trade-union leaders were "ins," too. And all those who were privileged perceived that if the soldiers saw themselves as being "outs," then what of the urban unemployed and those primary school dropouts who would have been glad for the salary of a lowly private? These are truly the "outs." Once the dam burst, once the legitimacy of government was entirely pushed aside and Nyerere's person removed, where would the demands of the "outs" end? And who could draw the line again between "ins" and "outs"? Thus, even if there were middle-level leaders who had grievances, this was not the base of support they wished and the demands of the mutineers were not the issues they wanted to exploit. In January, 1964, there were no revolutionaries in Dar es Salaam willing to use a mutinous army to call forth the urban unemployed and the rural underemployed.[51] Rank-and-file trade-union members were themselves privileged, since a fraction of Tanganyika population are wage-earners. While they wanted higher pay and more rapid advancement, they were also not unaware of the existence and dangers of an unemployed mob.

The Kenya and Uganda mutinies probably were nipped in the bud too quickly for any overt support to have developed for the soldiers among dissidents (and both countries had an ample share of oppositionists). Kenya, the most urbanized and industrialized of the East African countries, had (and still has) the most severe unemployment problem. Its own trade-union federation was fractionalized. Moreover, there was land hunger in Kenya; the area around Lanet Barracks was a sensitive one in this respect because it was an area of European settlement. There was no indication that grievances became more intense on these issues after the mutiny, which would have been the case if the soldiers had been identified with or if political groups had been willing to exploit the soldiers' demands for their own purposes. Uganda had its share of profound social cleavage which had been aggravated by the desire of the UPC government to move toward a one-party system.[52] But the opposition Democratic Party and Kabaka Yekka were not inclined to try to make cause with or capital out of the mutiny. Rather, they saw a weakening of an arm of the government. This arm could not be harnessed to their own ends, but it could not so easily be used against them either.

Because the Armies of East Africa were not highly visible in the capitals, much less in the country as a whole, and because they were seen to be British-organized Armies—mercenary Armies, as it were —they were thought of not as national bodies. Thus, there was little or no identification with them before or during the mutinies. When British troops came into East Africa, the situation changed. Independent African governments had called in the former colonial ruler. These governments were already sensitive to their vulnerability on the issue of economic progress. (Immediately after the mutiny a Tanganyika government statement insisted that, "Neither the people nor their Government have ever failed to stress the need for economic and social advance as a corollary to independence, and the whole people are mobilized for this purpose."[53] Later on the Minister for Finance said that the legitimate grievances of our soldiers were "part of the grievances of all our people which is poverty."[54] Now they faced attacks on their own independence and on racial grounds. It was not inconceivable that in the future the Armies would be seen as the carriers of nationalism who had been struck down by the British.[55] Thus, the nature of military force reconstruction became a most immediate and sensitive political problem, especially in Tanganyika.

In Uganda and Kenya, the entire army had not been so thoroughly implicated. In Uganda mutineers were dismissed and transported home. In Kenya, about 170 soldiers were eventually dismissed and another 100 court-martialed. (In Tanganyika, the death penalty was sought by the government for a number of men, but the harshest penalties were fifteen years for Sergeant Ilogi and ten years for some others.) It was only in Tanganyika that the Army had to be thoroughly reconstructed, since neither battalion could be relied on. The reconstruction of the Tanganyika Army and the aftermath of the mutinies in all three countries provide almost as much insight about the political systems of East Africa and the place of the military forces in them as the mutinies themselves.

THE AFTERMATH OF THE MUTINIES

WHEN they occurred, the mutinies seemed to be events of major importance. Although Prime Ministers Obote and Kenyatta de-emphasized them, Mr. Nyerere spoke openly of the catastrophic consequences of the Tanganyika revolt. He feared that Tanganyika's image of stability had been shattered. However, as attention shifted inside Tanganyika to the union with Zanzibar and the Five Year Plan and then to a new Constitution for party and state, the events of January seemed less significant. Similarly, in Kenya and Uganda, new events and crises came to the fore. But the significance of the Army mutinies did not diminish.

The attempt to build and rebuild military forces in East Africa has become entangled in cold war politics and to some extent in a growing rivalry among the East African countries. This development is only partially a result of the mutinies themselves. Internal rivalries in Kenya have centered around the Army as political leaders have sponsored their supporters for training abroad and have tried to gain control of the military force; these leaders have, in turn, been associated with and aided by various external powers. In Uganda, the intervention of the Army in the Congo fighting brought the Army into greater prominence, and the subsequent use of the Army to end the power of the Kabaka of Uganda and President of Uganda, Sir Edward Mutesa, made it clear that the present UPC government's power rests on the Army's support. So far, the Army does not seem to have a clear political complexion in terms of international alignments or domestic policies in Uganda or Kenya. But in both, the training and equipment of the Armies have become issues between domestic political factions. The importance of the mutinies in this regard is that they highlighted the power of the Armies and their unreliability, as well as the need to reconstruct them. Thus, the strengthening of the Armies and their entanglement in both domestic and international imbroglios takes place against the background of the past mutiny, not to mention the coups elsewhere in Africa.

Tanganyika provides us once again with the greatest insight, for there the attempt to build a new security force has become most entangled in different and rival foreign programs in Zanzibar and Tanganyika. It is in Tanganyika also that the most striking attempt is being made to politicize and nationalize the Army while tying it to the ruling party.

Immediately after the landing of British troops on January 25,

Nyerere called for a new army to be built around the TANU Youth League (TYL); but by February 12, Vice-President Kawawa was saying that the Youth League was "another nation-building group" but that it lacked leadership. A new category—National Servicemen—would provide leadership. TYL members would be recruited into special village centers and the National Servicemen would be leaders of such centers.[56] Youth League members flocked to be recruited into the National Service. Local TANU secretaries used the promise of an Army job to get people to take out TANU cards or to pay back dues. (Some of the people who were promised by local secretaries that they would enter the Army were patently physically unfit.) Recruitment was carried out by traveling teams, which would view men gathered by the regional police officers and the regional commissioners. John Nzunda, simultaneously Deputy Secretary General of TANU and Parliamentary Secretary, and other parliamentary secretaries also recruited. Noncommissioned officers who had been loyal took part too.

After the mutiny, many TANU Youth League members eventually were recruited into the Army. Political loyalty was a definite factor in recruitment, but the idea of enrolling TANU Youth League members at TANU offices to form a new Army was not sustained. It was found necessary to put forward the more encompassing concept of the National Service. These criteria emerged: new recruits for military forces must be citizens aged eighteen to twenty-five and unaccompanied by family. They must be able to read and write Swahili. Infantry officers must have completed Standard XII (the equivalent of high school).

In a change of portfolios in May, 1964, defense became the responsibility of the Vice-President, Mr. Kawawa. Both the National Service and Youth sections and the headquarters of the Tanzanian People's Defense forces are part of his portfolio.[57] A regular Army of four battalions and an air wing are being formed.[58] Individuals join the National Service. After three months of National Service training which includes taking part in nation-building activities, such as bush clearing or road construction, recruits are given the opportunity for selection by the Army or police.[59] Or they may choose to enter a specialist unit for paramilitary training in the last six months of their two years' training. Those who do not enter the Armed Forces are to establish new village settlements and stay on as settlers if they wish. They may be recalled for military duty. Initially, it was stated that all young men would be liable for National Service duty. But limited funds restrict the numbers of National Servicemen to about 3,300 during the Five Year Plan period of 1964–1969.

The government has adopted a number of measures aimed at ensuring political loyalty of the Armed Forces and integrating the Army with TANU. All members of the military and the police can now join TANU. On June 24, 1964, Vice-President Kawawa told recruits that they were citizens of the country and could participate fully in the politics of the United Republic. Mr. Kawawa told the recruits that the practice of refusing soldiers the right to participate in the politics of their countries was introduced by the colonialists.[60] (However, the independent Tanganyika government took three years to change this rule.)

Police and soldiers have enrolled en masse in response to the opening of TANU. In fact, they enroll as whole units. Company commanders are heads of the TANU committee established in the company. Officers are expected to do party liaison work and to explain to the troops their role in Tanzania's development.

An Honorary Commission in the People's Defense Forces with a rank of colonel was granted by President Nyerere to S. J. Kitundu, the Coast Regional Commissioner and a resident of Dar es Salaam. Mr. Kitundu was also appointed by the President as Political Commissar of the Tanzania Defense Forces, effective November 6, 1964. This post is not a listed position of the Ministry of Defense. It is designed to give a TANU official a high Army position. But so far Mr. Kitundu has had no operational direction of the Armed Forces.

Before the mutiny, TANU Youth Leaguers were often required to police meetings, to set up formal roadblocks to prevent smuggling, and even to collect taxes. In certain places, TANU personnel did constabulary work. These informal and irregular procedures have now been formalized.[61] To prepare them to "defend Tanganyika in the event of the country being attacked," members of the nation's Police Force, Prisons Service, National Service, and TANU Youth League are to undergo full military training with modern weapons. A reserve force for national defense is to be created.[62] A Field Force of militarized police will exist in each region. Also, special village police consisting of volunteers working under two regular policemen will be posted to villages, particularly those where there was occasional trouble, such as border areas.[63] People are told that their obligation is to help these police and act as citizen-police-helpers. It remains to be seen whether such a national reserve will come into being as an effective force. Villages that are in fact sparsely settled areas, spread out for miles, are hard to police. And Tanganyika has had one of the smallest salaried police forces in the world in relation to the population and the size of the country. To rectify this situation, there has been established a Special Constabulary of volunteers who undergo training for police work. Special Constables have been recruited from the TANU Youth League. Most regions have such a force, but it is best organized in Dar es Salaam where there are almost 250 uniformed Special Constables and over sixty Women Constables.

None of these measures guarantees a loyal and pliable security force. An Army with a large element of politically aware youth from the TANU Youth League may be difficult for the leadership to control. The TANU Youth League has been troublesome in the past and there have been sporadic attempts at governmental control by incorporating the Youth League into a Ministry of Culture and Youth. However, the Youth League has retained its identity. There already have been difficulties in the Army since the mutiny, although these have not been related to the new recruits. The government decided to accept some of the disgraced mutineers back into the Army as a stopgap measure when the Congo border situation became very tense. Shortly thereafter, there was trouble in the Army which has not been explained.[64] There were also rumors that a Zanzibar unit which was shipped to the southern region near Mozambique was undisciplined and had to be shipped back.

Aside from the difficulties in building a loyal and stable force, the Tanzanian government has problems in financing and training its security forces. The training of this force has created international incidents. President Nyerere's decision to accept a Chinese training team for his Army provoked warnings and outrage in the West. The President replied that the maximum risk was that the Army would revolt, which had already occurred with an Army that was not Chinese-trained. Other countries had refused his requests. Nyerere's reply was understandable, but in the meantime his military helpers could hardly be more varied. Israel now helps with the National Service; and West Germany was training an air wing before a crisis in West German-Tanzanian relations, after which Canada took over this training. Meanwhile, the Zanzibar units received Chinese, East German, and Soviet training and equipment. Not only do these arrangements pose technical difficulties for training, but Tanzanian security is related to international politics in a very marked way.

Nonetheless, it is clear that Tanzania intends to have a security establishment closely tied to TANU. The different militarized forces are designed to guard against any one branch repeating the January mutiny. But the government is not primarily worried about overt force being directed against it from within; it is worried about its own inability to exert force internally.

In other words, the central problem of the TANU government is: How can it assert itself in Tanganyika in the countryside? The National Service, the TANU Youth League, the Field Force of Military Police, and the special village police are all attempts to make the central will felt through creating new organizational forms. Another characteristic response has been the merging of TANU organizations and the defense forces. This tendency can be considered as politicizing the security forces. But perhaps it is more useful to see the enrolling of Army and police in TANU and the creating of defense TANU units as an attempt to strengthen TANU. A parallel with the entrance of civil service into TANU is clear. By incorporating these functional units, TANU does not so much extend its control—for the TANU center is limited in its ability to do this with its own territorial organizations—as give itself more concrete meanings and manifestations. TANU's functions are diffuse. They became specific by incorporating functionally specific organizations. TANU lacks executive and administrative personnel, so it recruits civil servants, policemen, and soldiers.

All groups and individuals must be within TANU so that no group or individual can threaten it from outside. TANU leaders feel that separatisms can be contained inside the party's embrace. They believe that the major difficulty with the Army that mutinied was that the Army was outside TANU. It was not informed about TANU goals and did not have contact with TANU leaders.[65] It remains to be seen whether the new Army proves a more reliable instrument.

CONCLUSIONS

THE stark facts of life in Tanganyika were driven home by the mutiny. The center was basically cut off from the rest of the country geographically and politically. Fewer than a thousand armed men could bring the government down, but the TANU organizations outside Dar es Salaam could keep "ruling." The Army mutiny illustrated the discontinuities between the center and the districts. It also illuminated a paradox in Tanganyika: The very absence of central political control has permitted a relatively stable situation in the countryside. The turmoil in Dar es Salaam during the mutiny, the subsequent concerns of East African federation and planning, and the strains of international politics did not much touch the countryside.

And here is the major lesson of the mutinies in Kenya and Uganda, as well as Tanganyika: It is easy to end civilian governments in Africa. They can be disbanded in capitals with little trouble, given the concerted effort of a single battalion. But so far no Army has ruled a tropical African country for even a few years and has exerted as much central authority, keeping the degree of public order that governments led by party leaders did prior to their removal. Perhaps Army administrations will be more successful with the problems of economic development and national integration than their civilian predecessors. But there is little concrete evidence on which to base this sanguine prediction. In fact, there is reason to believe that Army leaders who have little power at their disposal in terms of equipment and personnel will not be able to make up in force what they lack in legitimacy.

In East Africa, the mutinies were not military take-overs in conventional terms. They could not become so in the absence of military alliances with civilian groups and particularly with elements of the ruling parties. The Armies of Kenya, Tanganyika, and Uganda lacked one of the most important properties of a bona fide Army; they were without an indigenous officer corps. Their small size and relative lack of firepower and mobility would not have prevented their "taking over" in the sense of occupying the capital city. But they could not hope to rule even to the extent that civilian governments had ruled. Thus, there was no hope of attaining legitimacy through effectiveness. The mutinies themselves weakened the legitimacy of the military, although esteem was partially restored for them by British intervention.

Whether or not the East African militaries try to engage in either take-overs or coalitions with the parties now ruling or with some other political group depends on many factors. These factors pertain to developments within the military, within civilian elites, the relationship between them, and the way problems arise and are solved or not solved in society. In Tanganyika, TANU hopes to tie the military to the ruling party by suffusing it with TANU goals, by close supervision of the Army by political leaders, and by division of power among military and quasi-military branches. In Uganda, a community of interests is being assumed between a segment of the UPC leadership and the Army leadership based on common ethnic groupings and a mutual hostility to Buganda separatism. In Kenya, a change in recruitment in favor of the two largest tribes, Luo and Kikuyu, and military involvement in the north against Somalis is expected to maintain civilian leadership.

None of these attempts guarantees civilian supremacy in the future. Now that the East African Armies are officered by Africans they present a different, and somewhat unknown, quantity. The past mutinies can influence in different ways. They showed how easy it is to stage a coup; and since 1964, the numerous coups elsewhere in Africa have reinforced this example. But the mutinies also cast Armies into disrespect, and East African officers may be at pains to show that their Armies are disciplined and reliable. This resolve may weaken, should civilian regimes be unable to handle particular crises or have to call on the Army, as did the Uganda government when it ended the Presidency of the Kabaka of Buganda. Our views here are speculative. What we do know is that the East African Armies could intervene to bring down their governments, should they be so motivated. But we also know that they will run into all the difficulties of power and legitimacy already described. The mutinies revealed the real limits on military intervention in East Africa.

NOTES

1. The countries referred to are those in Tropical or Black Africa.

2. It seems to me that Aristide Zolberg means by "political order" the creation of an institutional order which is defined by effective political instruments. See Zolberg, Aristide, *Creating Political Order: The Party-States of West Africa,* Rand McNally and Co., Chicago, 1965, chap. 4, pp. 93–127.

3. The Congo has seemed to observers to be a unique or vastly exaggerated example of disorder and disunity in Africa. Recently the argument has been advanced that the Congo is not unique, but that African political systems are characterized by unintegrated sets of elites and that the type of disorder associated with the Congo is likely to emerge elsewhere. See Young, Crawford, "The Congo and Uganda: A Comparative Assessment," paper presented at the Ninth Annual Meeting of the African Studies Association, Bloomington, Indiana, October 26–29, 1966. See also Zolberg, Aristide, "A View from the Congo," *World Politics,* vol. 19, no. 1, October, 1966, pp. 137–149.

4. For a discussion of authoritative allocation of values, see Easton,

David, *The Political System,* Alfred A. Knopf, Inc., New York, 1953; and his *A Framework for Political Analysis,* Prentice-Hall, Englewood Cliffs, N.J., 1965.

5. It is interesting that the feudal periods in Europe are not generally characterized as anarchic but as the restoration of order after a period of breakdown of all order—the Dark Ages. Present American policy makers support the continuation of African political units in their present territorial form. The thread of the United States Congo policy is the commitment to the maintenance of central government. There is a mistrust of "overcentralization," where it cannot work, as in the Congo, Nigeria, and even in more seemingly homogeneous entities. But a breakup of these entities would be seen as a regression from the model of the national state toward a less civilized type, which existed in some former period.

6. This may be more than lip service. A commitment to civilian rule on the part of the military can also stem from a perception of the difficulties of ruling. General Ankrah of Ghana has wondered out loud about the personal benefits of being a ruler.

7. Morris Janowitz in *The Military in the Political Development of New Nations* (University of Chicago Press, Chicago, 1964, p. 44) uses the phrase "reservoir of legitimate authority" in his discussion of characteristics and potentialities of the military in new states. Undoubtedly, the legitimacy of the military as a ruling group is affected by the nature of the military's intervention. As Janowitz points out, it is important to distinguish military interventions as to whether they are "designed" or "reactive." That is, do the military intervene with positive and premeditated intent, or do they react to civilian weakness and even civilian pressure on them to intervene? *Ibid.,* pp. 16, 85, 113.

8. *Ibid.,* p. 33.

9. Nigeria's cases of corruption in the military have been on a grand scale. Three officers of the Nigerian Navy embezzled nearly 10 per cent of the 1964 Naval budget. Bell, M. J. V., *Army and Nation in Sub-Saharan Africa,* Adelphi Paper No. 21. Institute of Strategic Studies, London, August, 1965, p. 2.

Ranking Ugandan officers have been involved in lurid stories of smuggling ivory and gold and using Uganda's involvement in the Congo for their own benefit.

10. W. F. Gutteridge's "Introduction" to Wood, David, *The Armed Forces of African States,* Adelphi Paper No. 27, Institute of Strategic Studies, London, April, 1966, p. 2.

11. J. Kirk Sale in "The Generals and the Future of Africa" argues that this is true for Ghana and other African countries. *The Nation,* March 21, 1966, pp. 317–318.

12. In other words, the East African examples give us a chance to test the propositions about the military in new states that Janowitz puts forward in *The Military in the Political Development of New Nations* as he singles out the critical variables: organizational format, skill structure and career

lines, social recruitment and education, professional and political ideology, social cohesion, and political intervention. *Op. cit.,* pp. 27–29.

13. Shils, Edward, "The Military in the Political Development of New States," in Johnson, John J., editor, *The Role of the Military in Underdeveloped Countries.* Princeton University Press, Princeton, N.J., 1962, pp. 53–54.

14. The present commander of the Ugandan Army, Colonel Amin, has been a soldier for twenty years. He served in Burma as a private and was promoted to sergeant major after World War II. After Uganda's independence, he became a captain and subsequently received further promotions.

15. Officers in the Sudan are almost all from north of the Sahara but they have been on the scene longer than most African officers. Ethiopia, too, has some long-term officers. There are, of course, some traditional military elites, for example, in northern Nigeria and parts of Mali.

16. The following sketch of the size and composition of defense forces in Kenya, Uganda, and Tanganyika is drawn from a number of sources: *A Handbook of African Affairs,* edited by Helen Kitchen (Frederick A. Praeger, New York, 1964, pp. 205–206, 225–226, 228–229), reproduces data published in *Africa Report,* January, 1964. Harvey Glickman's "Impressions of Military Policy in Tanganyika" (RAND Corporation, November, 1963) and his *Some Observations on the Army and Political Unrest in Tanganyika* (Duquesne University Press, Pittsburgh, 1964) have been consulted for material on Tanganyika. I have also used East African press reports, government documents, and interviews carried out during 1963–1965 in East Africa. Data on the size and composition of the East African defense forces as of 1966 can be found in David Wood's *The Armed Forces of African States* (*op. cit.*) and in *Reference Handbook of the Armed Forces of the World,* edited by Lawrence L. Ewing and Robert C. Sellers; Robert C. Sellers and Associates, Washington, 1966.

17. Kenya also had more British officers than Tanganyika or Uganda. East Africans began to enter Mons Officer Training School and Sandhurst only after 1957. By 1963 there were Tanganyikan, Kenyan, and Ugandan officers; but British officers still held top command positions. However, by then East Africans were taking officer training courses in Israel as well as in Britain.

18. The size of the Buganda forces was constitutionally set with a ceiling of 650 men of all ranks. Buganda could not unilaterally change the size. The governments of Buganda and Uganda never reached agreement on the proper strength of the former's force; nor was agreement reached over the precise powers of the Uganda Central Government's Inspector-General of Police over the Kabaka of Buganda's police. This issue, among others, was still outstanding in May, 1966, when Uganda Army units shelled the Kabaka's Palace and fought his police force, which defended it.

The tribal composition of the Uganda police mirrored the tribal composition of the Army in that recruitment was predominantly from northern Nilotic tribes rather than from southern Bantu tribes. The Acholi, Iteso, and Lango were represented in the Army and police by more than their share of the Uganda population. See *Annual Report of the Uganda Police,* The Government Printer, Entebbe, 1961, p. 4.

19. See also Julius Nyerere's *The Second Scramble* (Tanganyika Standard Limited, Dar es Salaam, 1962) in which he downgraded the idea of a Tanganyikan Army in favor of a UN or African Army.

20. Tanganyika has restricted labor inflows from Kenya. In 1965 a Uganda Army convoy picked up military equipment in Tanganyika and crossed the Kenya border on the way back to Uganda without Kenyan permission, causing an imbroglio between Kenya and her East African neighbors.

21. Tanganyika is hardly "a country with as few external and internal security problems as, say in Africa," given these circumstances. Bell, M. J. V., *op. cit.,* p. 4.

22. Leys, Colin, "Violence in Africa," *Transition,* vol. 5, no. 21, 1965, pp. 17–20.

23. *Ibid.,* p. 19.

24. TANU is the ruling party in the Tanganyika part of the United Republic of Tanzania. The Afro-Shirazi Party rules in Zanzibar.

25. Glickman, Harvey, *Some Observations on the Army and Political Unrest in Tanganyika, op. cit.,* p. 5.

26. *Ibid.*

27. KANU won an electoral victory in May, 1963, after the KADU-KANU coalition was dissolved. A number of former KADU leaders were absorbed into the KANU leadership.

28. The Kamba leader, Paul Ngei, has alternately been in and out of KANU governments.

29. See my article, "The Party and the No-Party State: Tanganyika and the Soviet Union," *Transition,* vol. 3, no. 13, 1964, pp. 25–33.

30. Colin Leys, in "Recent Relations Between the States of East Africa" (*International Journal,* vol. 20, no. 4, 1965, pp. 510–523), has argued that the time factor in East Africa was crucial by 1963. Tanganyika had been independent for more than two years, Uganda more than one; and Kenya was just becoming independent. Moreover, Tanganyika was a political and economic vacuum. Uganda had relatively strong social, economic, and political subsystems within the national political system. Kenya had problems of a white majority, the confrontation of large tribal groups, and urban unemployment.

31. Bell (*op. cit.*) points out that it was not the forthcoming requirements of independence, which was not contemplated in 1955, that prompted the French to undertake this crash program to upgrade the manpower reserves of *Afrique Noire.*

32. In the following account of the East African mutinies I have drawn on my own "National Security in Tanganyika after the Mutiny," *Transition,* vol. 5, no. 21, 1965, pp. 39–46. I have also made use of a very comprehensive account compiled by Christopher Hobson of the University of Chi-

cago Department of Political Science, based on newspapers and journals and on his own first-hand experience.

33. Kyle, Keith, "Mutinies and After," *The Spectator,* no. 7075, January 31, 1964, p. 139. Kavona was appointed second in command by the President after order was restored. Some months later he was put under preventive detention. No explanation was given then or since. His earlier actions may have been held against him, and it was rumored that he was involved with dissident troops later on.

34. The request for more money involved a demand for a raise in base pay for privates from about $15 per month to more than $37 per month.

35. Police in many African countries have taken this position during Army coups or internal Army struggles.

36. See "The Brushfire in East Africa, from January 1 to February 13, 1964," *Africa Report,* vol. 9, no. 2, February, 1964, p. 21.

37. One report said that Captain Sarakikya was being marched at bayonet point to a cell in Tabora when the signal appointing him commanding officer came through from Dar es Salaam. He ordered the mutineers to desist and took control; and he supervised the shipping out of British officers and noncommissioned officers. *Tanganyika Standard,* Dar es Salaam, January 30, 1964, p. 5.

38. When asked in a press conference on January 23 what action would be taken against the mutineers, he ended the meeting without answering.

39. On January 25, Sarakikya had withdrawn arms from his troops in Tabora. But British paratroopers landed there anyway and took control of the town. At Nachingwea, where a company had been facing the Mozambique border, Army troops who had asserted themselves in the town surrendered to local police.

40. The fact that the Army appeared well organized in Dar es Salaam and the chain effect of the Dar mutiny gave rise to rumors about foreign intervention. Chou En-lai was about to visit Tanganyika, and China was specifically mentioned as an instigator of the difficulties. There appears to have been no truth to these rumors. On January 27, the Tanganyika government issued a press statement that the revolt was not connected with outside subversion and noted that it was not in any way communist-inspired. Then on January 30, the government felt compelled to deny that the implication of the January 27 statement was that the mutiny was connected with any popular movement.

41. From 1957 to 1960 there had been an East African Land Force connected with the old East African High Commission. The East African Common Service Organization replaced the High Commission in 1960, but it did not take on defense coordination. And with independence each country became responsible for its defense, even in the area of administration where the High Command had some responsibilities. There was a common East African Navy, but within a week of Tanganyika's independence, it was announced that the East African Navy would be disbanded. The East African Defense Committee was disbanded in October, 1963. See

Johns, David, "Defense and Police Organization in East Africa," paper presented to East Africa's Institute of Social Research Conference, December, 1963.

42. The organization of the Zanzibar Revolution, the role of particular individuals, the amount of outside support, and the part played by Tanganyikans remain very murky still.

43. Trade-union leaders took up the cry and said the President's policy was contrary to Africanization. One representative of the Local Government Workers Union said that Nyerere was taking Tanganyika back to colonial days. See *Tanganyika Standard*, January 9, 1964, p. 3. Toward the end of 1963, the Grand Council of the Tanganyika Federation of Labour had rejected the government's proposal to integrate the TFL with the government. When the British landed troops at the end of January, certain trade-union leaders were arrested and incarcerated under the Preventive Detention Act. Some trade-union leaders did go out to Colito Barracks during the mutiny to encourage the troops and politicize demands. However, the government arrested some on grounds of national security, although they did not support the mutiny but simply opposed the government's trade-union policy.

44. Ginwala, Frene, "The Tanganyika Mutiny," *World Today*, vol. 20, no. 3, March, 1964, pp. 93–97.

45. Kyle, Keith, *loc. cit.*

46. *Africa Report, loc. cit.*

47. This occurred at a meeting of the *Umoja Wa Wanawake*, or Women's League. See *Tanganyika Standard*, January 30, 1964, p. 1.

48. Austin Shaba, Minister for Local Government, who was in London during the mutiny. See *Tanganyika Standard*, January 30, 1964, p. 5.

49. See *Uganda Argus,* Kampala, February 13, 1964, for Mr. Nyerere's remarks.

50. Chief Fundikira even rejoined TANU and took his place once again in the Tanganyika Parliamentary Party to show his solidarity after the mutiny.

51. If any Zanzibar leaders were so inclined, they were either preoccupied in Zanzibar or judiciously quiet.

52. See *Tanganyika Standard*, January 8, 1964, p. 1.

53. *East African Standard*, Nairobi, January 31, 1964, p. 1.

54. *Sunday News,* Dar es Salaam, February 7, 1964, p. 7.

55. Hobson reports that in a straw poll he conducted among high school students largely living in Temeke, an outlying industrial section of the capital, 75 per cent opposed the calling in of Britain and better than 50 per cent thought the Army's mutiny had been justified. It is very probable that the fact of British intervention affected subsequent views about the Army mutiny, although I have no "before" and "after" data to support this theory.

56. *Tanganyika Standard,* February 12, 1964, p. 5.

57. Tanganyika's and Zanzibar's Armies are now merged in the Tanzanian Defense Force. I do not know whether this is effective operationally.

58. Three battalions will be in Tanganyika and one in Zanzibar. Plans to form a Navy have been announced.

59. Wood reports that half of Army personnel is to consist of volunteers from National Service. *Op. cit.,* p. 18.

60. *Nationalist,* Dar es Salaam, June 25, 1964, p. 2.

61. The Reserve Forces Bill legalizes paramilitary training and functions of the TYL.

62. The reserve is to be made up of 4,000 volunteers. Wood, *loc. cit.*

63. *Reporter,* Nairobi, February 12, 1965; *Nationalist,* February 2, 1965, p. 1.

64. The September 12, 1964, headline of the *Nationalist* read: "U.R. (United Republic) Army Arrests." The text of a government announcement was printed: "In active pursuance of its duty to maintain the integrity and safety of the United Republic the Government yesterday found it necessary to arrest and detain a small number of servants of the Republic. This number included officers and other ranks of the United Republic Army, who were of doubtful loyalty and guilty of insubordination by default." It was on this occasion that Elisha Kavona was arrested.

65. Interviews.

Military Intervention in the
New States of Tropical Africa:
Elements of Comparative Analysis*

by ARISTIDE R. ZOLBERG

ALTHOUGH it is easy to account for the recent wave of army coups in the new states of tropical Africa[1] by examining the characteristics of each country's military establishment and the particular political and economic situation at the time of the take-over, it is impossible to specify variables which distinguish *as a class* countries where coups have occurred from others which have so far been spared. Until the middle of January, 1966, the wave of coups seemed to be a characteristic of French-speaking countries. On the whole, these countries are poorly endowed economically (except for the Congo-Kinshasa, formerly Leopoldville); they have weak political institutions; and their political life had been characterized since independence either by the persistence of factional and ethnic politics (as in the Congo or Dahomey), or by the appearance of a deceptive "one-party system," which merely papered over persistent political cracks (as in Upper Volta or the Central African Republic).

---

* Although this paper is not based on first-hand field observation of military regimes, the discussion of political systems in the first part stems from earlier studies based on field work in West and East Africa in 1959–1960 and 1964. Many of the ideas are contained in my book, *Creating Political Order: The Party-States of West Africa,* Rand McNally and Co., Chicago, 1966, and in "A View from the Congo," *World Politics,* vol. 19, no. 1, October, 1966, pp. 137–149. My analysis of military interventions and military rule is based exclusively on secondary sources. Unless otherwise specified, data are drawn from reports in *West Africa* (London, weekly); *Afrique Nouvelle* (Dakar, weekly); *Le Monde, Sélection Hebdomadaire* (Paris, weekly); *The Times* (London); *The New York Times; Jeune Afrique* (Tunis, weekly); and *Africa Report* (Washington, monthly). I am very grateful to Messrs. Christopher Hobson and Ronald Bayer, graduate

Although the Nigerian affair of mid-January suddenly expanded the category to include an English-speaking West African country, long thought to be among the best prepared for independence and a leading hope for democracy, an important category of countries still appeared to be immune: the party-states of West Africa, where nationalist leaders had transformed their movements into organizational weapons which provided a basic institutional apparatus for political modernization. The February, 1966, coup in Ghana dealt a serious blow to any attempt at multivariate analysis. What do Mauritania, Senegal, the Gambia, Mali, Guinea, Ivory Coast, Cameroon, Chad, Niger, Gabon, Rwanda, Kenya, Uganda, Tanzania, Zambia, and Malawi have in common, compared to the other newly independent states, except that so far there has been no successful military challenge to the authority of their leaders? And if Gabon, Kenya, Uganda, and Tanzania are excluded, because we do not know what the consequences of military coups or mutinies would have been if the former colonial power had not intervened to bolster the challenged regime, do the remainder constitute a coherent grouping?

The major theme of this study is that military coups are likely to occur *anywhere* in the region because of fundamental and lasting characteristics of political life. Whether or not a major military intervention occurs in a given African country at a particular time is related to highly specific and circumstantial features of that country's current political situation, rather than to any basic deviant political characteristics. Furthermore, I shall suggest that military interventions (successful or unsuccessful) are but one aspect of a more general phenomenon, the importance of force and of the coup de force in African political life, and that this phenomenon is itself related to persistent patterns of African politics. Hence, it might be most fruitful from the point of view of comparative analysis to attempt a general examination relating military interventions to the political environment. An understanding of this context is important not only to analyze the process of military intervention itself, but also to appreciate the situation which military elites must face *after* they have assumed responsibility for government. From this point of view, although military take-overs are important events, they

students in political science at the University of Chicago, who have prepared detailed background analyses of military interventions in Tanganyika, Uganda, Kenya, Ghana, and Nigeria. I am deeply indebted to Professor Morris Janowitz who invited me to prepare this paper and has long been a source of inspiration for my ventures in comparative macrosociology.

constitute but minor disturbances which are unlikely to bring about significant changes in the overall patterns of political life in the new African states.

AUTHORITY, POWER, AND FORCE IN POST-INDEPENDENT AFRICA

IN THE light of later events, one is struck by the soundness of some of the hypotheses set forth by James S. Coleman and Belmont Bryce, Jr., in one of the first essays on the subject of the military in Sub-Saharan Africa, written several years before discussions of the likelihood of military interventions became commonplace.[2] Two items in particular are useful in the present context. Commenting on the small size and organizational weakness of the military establishments inherited by most countries from the colonial era, they pointed out that the Congo crisis of 1960 demonstrated "the determinative influence which a small military force could exercise in a situation in which countervailing institutions or power groups are absent."[3] Furthermore, discussing the overall pattern of civilian–military relationships, they indicated that although in the new African states the politicians, the bureaucracy, and the Army shared common national goals such as stability and order, national unity, and rapid modernization, "experience elsewhere indicates that, if the civilian regime becomes stalemated in its pursuit of these goals, there is a high probability that the military will intervene."[4]

The first statement stresses the importance of evaluating the military establishment's potential political role in relation to salient features of the political system, rather than in relation to its own intrinsic characteristics. It dramatizes the fact that although on the whole military institutions in Africa are among the least developed in the world, they operate in political systems which are characterized by weak structures.[5] If this institutional weakness is established, the conditions indicated in the second statement, "stalemate" in the pursuit of modernization, are bound to follow because any regime will have a very limited capability for leverage over its environment.

Together, these two propositions provide a basic paradigm for the understanding of African politics before and after military interventions. Yet, the paradigm appears to be deceptively simple. Hardly anyone would question its soundness in cases such as the Congo. But how can one speak of the absence of "countervailing institutions of power groups" in countries dominated by a "mobilizing" party such as the Convention People's Party (CPP) of Ghana, or by strong regional organizations, such as in Nigeria? If a power vacuum was so prevalent, why did even the most intelligent observers of the African scene stress the danger of too much authority, rather than of the absence of authority? Although the overall soundness of the paradigm seems confirmed by later events, the propositions it contains require explanation. I shall attempt to demonstrate that although there were significant variations among the regimes established during the period of decolonization and at the time of independence, *these variations occurred within a relatively narrow range.* Although studies of African politics have tended to focus on differences between political patterns and on the elaboration of typologies, scholars have neglected rather basic similarities which can be understood by briefly reviewing the circumstances of the birth of the new states.

It has often been stated that African countries are "artificial creations." Although such statements sometimes ignore the importance of the political communities defined by the colonial powers as major reference points for educated nationalists, as shown by the case of "Kamerun," an artifact of German colonialism which was dismembered after World War I but nevertheless continued to provide a rallying point for political demands several decades later, they do provide an important starting point. African states are peculiar entities because they were initially created when European conquerors carved out portions of an international system or subsystem constituted by the interacting societies of pre-European Africa into convenient administrative entities. From then on, these new units provided a territorial framework within which social, economic, political, and cultural changes that accompanied colonization began to constitute a new society. While this process occurred at varying rates and had reached different stages at about the time of independence, nowhere had it occurred sufficiently to enable us to characterize what was contained within these countries as a "society" in the normally accepted sociological sense of the term. The older societies had survived in part even where their existence was not legally recognized, as in countries administered under direct rule.

Furthermore, the new national society did not grow at the expense of the older societies contained within a given territory as in a zero-sum game. Instead, most countries can be viewed as a multilayered amalgam in which both types of societies coexist, with a certain degree of functional specialization between them in different spheres of social activity such as economics, politics, and religion. All individuals occupy certain roles in both types of society, with some almost totally uninvolved in the modern, national society (but affected by its existence) and some almost fully detached from traditional society.[6]

This overall image of the heterogeneous societies contained within the new African states provides the basis for an understanding of the special character of their political systems.[7] If we seek to determine how values are authoritatively allocated within these countries, it is evident that in every single case, the visible modern political institutions such as political parties and groups, central executive and legislative bodies, as well as the apparatus of territorial administration (which often includes party structures), deal with only a portion of the total allocative activity. The remainder must be allocated by other means and by other structures. This distinction is fairly obvious where some functional division of authority was provided for as part of the independence constitution, as in Nigeria or Uganda. But it is equally valid where traditional political structures have no recognized legal or political standing, or even where they have been formally abolished, as in Guinea or Mali. The argument is based primarily on negative evidence: even in African countries where central institutions claim a monopoly of allocative activity, the structures associated with this center, such as parties, legislative bodies, and secular courts, simply do not have the capacity to carry this load.[8] Hence, a common feature of all African political systems is the continued existence of a "residual sector" of relatively traditional political activity together with the more prominent relatively modern sector with which analysts are usually concerned.

Within the limits imposed by this fundamental feature shared by all the new states, there were some variations in political arrangements at the time of independence. Most of the literature on African politics has tended to use as a major classificatory variable the degree of competitiveness of the regime. Hence, a distinction has usually been made between one-party and multiparty countries, between the "revolutionary-centralizing" (or "mobilization") type and the "pragmatic-pluralistic" (or "reconciliation") type.[9] The Congo-Kinshasa has usually been viewed as a unique case, and little attention has been paid on the whole to the relatively large group of countries such as the Congo (Brazzaville), Upper Volta, or Dahomey. These had formally become "one-party states" when one of several competing ethnic-regional leagues became dominant as the result of a game of politics similar to that which at one time ensured the dominant position of Radical-Socialists in French governments. However, these African parties institutionalized this dominance by changing the rules of the game.[10]

However useful these classifications may have been initially, they tended to exaggerate differences between regimes by paying attention to ideological tone ("radicals," "moderates") and African pronouncements concerning the nature of their regimes ("the party penetrates every aspect of political life") at the expense of structural analysis based on healthy skepticism. Furthermore, most observers tended to become the prisoners of their conceptual categories: once a political organization was identified as a "mass party," for example, certain functional inferences were drawn from the operations of the structures usually associated with parties of this type in other parts of the world, regardless of whether these structures had in fact been institutionalized in a given African country. Yet, a careful empirical examination would reveal in almost every case that there was a wide gap between the organization model from which leaders derived their inspiration and their capacity to implement such schemes in reality. The case of Ghana is most instructive in this respect: although President Kwame Nkrumah attempted to transform the CPP into an organization which could control all aspects of Ghanaian life, the CPP eventually came to reflect many aspects of the country's social structure and almost ceased to exist as a distinct organization.

This process was by no means limited to parties, but occurred within bureaucracies as well, to such an extent that it would be much more appropriate in most cases to speak of "government employees" as a categoric group than of "bureaucracies" in the usual sociological sense of the word. Similarly, constitutional arrangements were not anchored in supporting norms or institutions, and hence had little reality beyond their physical existence as a set of written symbols deposited in a government archive. Trade unions, whether or not they were transformed into "party wings," were little more than intermittent congeries of urban employed and unemployed gathered together to protest an occasional government decision.[11]

Under these generally shared circumstances, it is not surprising that the Founding Fathers of most African states behaved very much in the same way in order to maintain themselves in office. Initially, benefiting from the sudden creation of a multitude of new political offices, from the departure of colonial officials, and from the expansion of state-directed economic activity which had begun during the latter years of welfare-state colonialism, as well as from the prevalent sense that they had earned the right to rule through their leadership of protest movements, they were able to construct adequate political machines based primarily on the distribution of benefits to individual and group claimants and on the construction of shifting coalitions. Although no African regime ever ceased to rely on this set of techniques, most of the regimes soon resorted to coercion as well. This was a crucial turning point because it brought to the fore the importance of instruments of force, such as the police and the military, with consequences to be discussed in the next section.

This shift to a new phase of political activity is related to two sets of reinforcing factors. First, it was due to the growing gap between the leaders' ideological aspirations and their capacity to implement the policies these aspirations entailed. Whether or not it is appropriate to speak of a "revolution of rising expectations" throughout the continent, there is little doubt that such a revolution has occurred among those responsible for government. Their commitment to rapid modernization is defined in a very specific, imitative manner, to include the creation of a homogeneous society, an effective bureaucracy, political acquiescence, and a rapidly progressing economy. Since most African countries are farther behind in most of these respects than any other set of countries in the world, governments with the lowest capability to rule have assumed the heaviest burdens. "Machine" techniques are inadequate for this purpose; instead, the society must be forced into acquiescence and into effective action. A major source of the vulnerability of African regimes thus stems from their own definition of the situation, since they can be criticized for failing to achieve objectives imposed not by outsiders but by themselves.

At the same time, however, most governments also face very serious threats to their self-maintenance. This was most obvious in the case of the Congo, where challenges stemming from every direction occurred simultaneously and most dramatically within a few weeks after independence: no government in the world, let alone that of Patrice Lumumba, could survive a mutiny of its Army, the secession of the richest part of the country, a severe interruption in the flow of tax revenue, and the loss of its bureaucratic cadre. Although in other countries, the challenges have been less extreme and have usually been spaced over a few years, their cumulative impact has not necessarily been much less severe. Everywhere, governments have been faced with some or all of the following, together or successively: a high incidence of social conflict stemming from the characteristically consistent cleavages which prevail throughout the country as a whole as the result of the uneven impact of modernization; the exacerbation of ethnic and regional rivalries as the result of the rapid extension of political participation shortly before independence and the heightened awareness of the importance of political stakes; deep antagonisms between political generations (and between "institutional" generations) as the result of the rapid filling of offices by relatively young men at first, while the production of new generations of qualified aspirants for these same offices was accelerated; the rapid growth of urbanization without concomitant growth in the economic system's absorptive capacity, leading to more or less permanent unemployment of individuals with minimal educational qualifications; relative deprivation among even the most privileged groups in the society, such as government employees, both civilian and military; widespread fluctuations in the world prices of primary commodities, on which the economies of most of these countries remain highly dependent; relative scarcity of investment capital and conflicting recipes for the maximization of return on aid.

Significantly, these are all structural factors which are relatively independent of the wisdom or devotion of particular political leaders. Although the incidence of human error and weakness, or of sheer roguishness, is probably not higher in Africa than elsewhere, there are so few degrees of freedom in these situations that the consequences of these factors are usually vastly magnified. For example, corruption among government officials, which probably did not interfere with the industrialization of Great Britain or the United States (and perhaps even facilitated it), can have very damaging consequences where it diverts a large proportion of very scarce resources from the provision of public facilities into the pockets of a "nonproductive" bureaucratic bourgeoisie.

On the whole, African leaders have tended to deal with these challenges by using coercion against individuals deemed responsible for the creation of disturbances. It is difficult to understand exactly why this became the usual pattern, except in reference to the cultural apparatus and personality characteristics of many leaders, which tend to combine to produce operational ideologies that explain departures from anticipated normal (favorable) situations through willful interference by "enemies." Within this cabalistic frame of mind, and in the face of growing insecurity, African leaders have intimidated, jailed, or exiled their opponents; they have declared increasingly broad areas of public life to be beyond the pale of debate and of bargaining; they have declared most categories of associations to be illegal; they have curtailed freedom of the press, of association, and of speech; they have ritualized loyalty and citizenship into conformity and subjection.

Although the growth of this trend has sometimes been taken to indicate the significant reinforcement of authority structures, this is an erroneous interpretation of what has been indeed a major transformation of African politics—the shift away from political power as a technique of rule to a reliance on force. At the same time, as African regimes have tended to deny to their opponents the right and the opportunity of using political power, they also have come to rely increasingly on force to express their demands.

This situation is an illustration of the more general relationship of "power" and "force" discussed by Talcott Parsons, who has suggested that they are related in much the same way as "money" is to "gold" in economically advanced societies. Although control over the monetary metal is centralized through central banking systems, the value of money is normally based on the productivity of the economy by means of a highly pyramidal system of credit rather than on the commodity value of gold, except in one special instance, that is, when there is a run on banks. Similarly, although modern governments have achieved a monopoly of "force," "power" is normally based on the overall social structure rather than on this monopoly. Furthermore, just as dollars in the bank "do double duty, remaining at the disposal of creditors while they are also at the disposal of borrowers," so in the case of power, "commitments to the performance of binding obligations are the analog of dollars and may be said to do double duty." Hence, "a 'power bank,' like a money bank, is, if it is functioning well, 'insolvent' at any given moment with respect to its formal obligations, in the sense that it cannot fulfill all its legitimate obligations if there is insistence on the fulfillment too rapidly."[13] If there develops an inflationary spiral of demands on the system to fulfill its obligations, the response can be twofold: "First, an increasingly stringent scale of priorities of what can and cannot be done will be set up; second, increasingly severe negative sanctions for noncompliance with collective decisions will be imposed."[14] Thus, a process of power-deflation occurs and force comes fully into play.

This is indeed the sort of transformation which seems to have occurred in most new African states within a few years of independence, and which has set the stage for military intervention. The link between this situation and the military can be suggested by means of the following proposition: *When a shift from power to force occurs, it is accompanied by a shift in the relative "market value" of existing structures: in the case of the new African states, the value of political parties and of civilian administration has undergone a sort of deflation, while the value of the police and of the military has been vastly increased. This occurs even when there is no actual deterioration in the operational effectiveness of one set of structures or an increase in the operational effectiveness of the other set.*

PATTERNS OF MILITARY INTERVENTION

IN THIS section, each country will continue to be considered as a separate political system, as in the preceding section. It is also necessary, however, to consider all of them together as units in an interacting international subsystem in order to account for the phenomenon of "waves" or "contagion" which seems to be an important aspect of military intervention throughout the continent.

Given a political situation such as the one we have discussed in the preceding section, in which the "market value" of even the weakest military establishments is greatly enhanced, the reliability of the rulers' monopoly of force becomes crucial. As Parsons has indicated, however, "Most important, whatever the physical technology involved, a critical factor in socially effective force is always the social organization through which it is implemented. There is always some degree of dependence on the loyalties of the relevant personnel to the elements of the social structure ostensibly controlling them."[15]

Paradoxically, then, rulers resort to force when power and legitimacy fail; but the use of force to implement authority enhances the problem of the legitimacy of the rulers in the eyes of those to whom the implementation must necessarily be entrusted. Attempts to balance one instrument of force which is thought to be unreliable (such as the regular army) by means of the creation of another (such as a presidential guard) or the reinforcement of quasi-military bodies (such as a party militia or the gendarmerie) merely modifies the problem of legitimacy but does not eliminate it. In fact, as seems to have been the case in many African countries, resort to this technique may exacerbate the situation and lead to a preemptive military coup.[16] The outlook of the military itself becomes a crucial variable, which can be analyzed in terms of its cognitive, affective, and evaluative components in relation to a given set of authorities, to a particular type of regime, and to their own position within the situation.

As African regimes came to rely increasingly on force to deal with challenges to their authority, the military rapidly learned how much weaker were the African rulers than their predecessors. Called upon repeatedly to put down strikes or to deal with disorder in a dissident region, being asked to support one faction of the government against another in a showdown (as in Senegal in December, 1962), participating in similar operations in a country other than their own (as in the case of the Ghanaian and Nigerian forces in the Congo), or merely acquiring information about the involvement of other military units in events of this sort, officers and men at all levels became acquainted more intimately than many others with the seamy side of political life in their own country and on the continent as a whole.[17] They also learned that control over even a small, ill-equipped, poorly trained body of men was crucial. Furthermore, as most regimes reduced consultation and representation, and groups tended to express their demands by direct action such as street demonstrations bordering on uprisings, the military learned that actions of this sort were often the only effective way of presenting demands and that they themselves were by virtue of their organizational characteristics the best-organized "trade union" in the country. Thus, the cognitive component of the military outlook underwent rapid change within a short time.

Their feelings toward the rulers of their own country, and more generally toward "politicians" as a class, also deteriorated rapidly. An examination of statements made by Army leaders who have intervened in politics strikingly reveals that this phenomenon is almost completely independent of "ideology," in the sense of the regime's policies in such areas as economic development or international affairs. Initially, most African regimes benefited from a certain degree of legitimacy as properly elected officials, as the leaders of nationalist movements, as the heirs of "tradition," or even as the legitimate successors of the former colonial power. But this legitimacy was eroded very rapidly for disparate reasons. They include serious departures from general continuity with the colonial order under which senior officers had been socialized (as in Ghana in the face of attempts to indoctrinate the troops to Nkrumahism, or in some French-speaking countries where a rapprochement with Communist China seems to have been resented by officers who served their apprenticeship fighting with the French in Indochina), or conversely, timidity in severing postindependence political or economic ties with the former colonial power (as in the Congo-Brazzaville, Gabon, or possibly in the second Mobutu coup of 1965).

Military contempt for the Founding Fathers has grown in the face of generalized corruption at the uppermost levels of government even while these same governments urged sacrifices at the lower levels and used force to deal with objections. The legitimacy of nationalist leaders as a whole has come into question when it became clear that many pursued partisan political advantage even in the face of permanent governmental instability, whether in a multiparty situation (as in Nigeria or Dahomey), or by means of factionalism in a one-party situation. Although military personnel, like other government employees, benefited on the whole from a privileged economic position, they were subject to a process of relative deprivation because their reference group was not the unfortunate mass of their countrymen, but rather those who, with qualifications similar to their own, were in a position to define the scale of privilege itself. The feelings of the military toward the politicians can be summarized as follows: they are corrupt, inept, backward, and unappreciative of the military. In some cases these negative feelings were directed toward a particular group of incumbent rulers; but when these had been displaced by others, often as the result of earlier military intervention, they tended to be extended to politicians as a class.

Given this understanding of the situation and their feelings toward the rulers, officers have come to believe that they alone can save the country from the politicians and have seldom hesitated to intervene directly in the political process. These interventions have taken several forms ranging from "strikes" and "demonstrations" on behalf of their own immediate interests, to "referee" interventions in order to settle conflicts, to complete "take-overs" with the intention of establishing a military-dominant regime or of sponsoring an acceptable regime manned by others. Although some interventions can easily be placed within one of these categories, these patterns should be viewed as *elements* in a given situation and are not necessarily mutually exclusive. A particular intervention sometimes contains several components, either concurrently or in succession. Yet, it is possible to distinguish an overall trend, both within each country and over the continent as a whole from beginning to end of the period under consideration: Military interventions have tended to move from either or both "strikes" and "referee" actions to "take-overs."

The "strike" element was prominent in the mutiny of the Force Publique in the Congo (July, 1960), and in the three East African mutinies of 1963, in the lesser known case of Niger (1963), and in the Congo-Brazzaville (July, 1966). Although none of these resulted in take-overs, the Congolese mutiny was a prelude for further interventions. What seems to have begun as a strike in Togo (1963) became a referee intervention when the President was "accidently" killed by a group of soldiers. On the other hand, the military coups in the Central African Republic and in Upper Volta (1966) contained important strike elements related in the first case to a rivalry between the gendarmerie and the Army for budgetary allocations and in the second, to Army solidarity with veterans.

"Referee" actions seem to fall into two distinct subtypes. One is a reaction to protracted conflict culminating in a total deadlock among politicians. This was the case, for example, when President Kasavubu and Premier Patrice Lumumba dismissed each other in August–September, 1960, and again when efforts by President Kasavubu to find a Premier to succeed Moise Tshombe failed in 1965. The other is a reaction to protracted conflict between a regime and trade unions, an ethnic–regional movement, or some other popular organization, in which the incumbent government ultimately decides to apply force in the settlement of the dispute. Faced with a choice between implementing the government's decision and becoming identified with it, or abstaining and exposing the government's impotence, the military more often than not chooses the latter course. This must not be taken as an indication that the military necessarily sympathizes with the dissenters, since their behavior after a successful intervention under these circumstances indicates a tendency to muzzle these same demands.[18] Examples of this pattern include the Congo-Brazzaville (1963), and Upper Volta (1966), where the military and the police at first assisted the government, then withdrew, and finally obtained its resignation on behalf of "the people." The three Soglo interventions in Dahomey (1963; November, 1965; and December, 1965) involved elements of both types of referee actions: a struggle between Hubert Maga, Sourou Migan Apithy, and Justin Ahomadegbe, leaders of regional-ethnic organizations in the North, the Southeast, and the Southwest respectively, as well as a long drawn-out dispute between the successive governments and labor organizations (including both employed and unemployed), stemming in part from the difficulty which Dahomey has experienced in absorbing its educated citizens expelled from other French-speaking African countries where they had long served as clerks and skilled workers when Dahomey was ahead of the others in educational development. The case of Nigeria is more complex, since it initially involved a coup by middle-ranking officers, and only later the assumption of executive authority by the Army's commander when the results of the coup appeared to threaten the country's survival as a unit. There is no doubt, however, that a precipitating factor was a decision by the coalition government, dominated by the North, to send in the Army (whose officers are mostly southerners) to pacify the Western Region where the struggle between South and North had reached the level of a near-civil war.

Referee interventions which occurred before 1965 tended to be directed against specific rulers rather than against civilian regimes as such and usually led to the establishment of a government of "national unity," composed of politicians from various factions or of technicians, with the Army in the background. But in 1965, referee interventions appeared to merge with military take-overs with the intention of establishing military rule. Often a first referee intervention had failed to bring about the desired result, as in the second Mobutu coup (1965), and possibly in the abortive attempts in Togo by the leader of the 1963 coup two years later, or in the equally unsuccessful attempt by the military in the Congo-Brazzaville (July, 1966) against the regime they had helped establish three years earlier. The other avenue to the establishment of military rule is the transformation of a referee action, usually when the military grows impatient with politicians as a class during negotiations to establish a government of "national unity," as seems to have been the case in Dahomey (1965), in the Central African Republic, and in Nigeria.

So far, Ghana provides the only instance of a military take-over clearly initiated by the Army and with the intention from the very beginning of substituting a new regime for the existing one. Since Nkrumah had been in power for fifteen years and since the CPP had come much closer, relatively speaking, to the establishment of a regime in Ghana than was the case in any of the other countries under consideration, it is possible that the Army and its police allies believed that a more powerful deterrent was necessary. Hardly anyone could be found within the country who had not been somehow associated with the regime.[19]

Although in each case of military intervention which leads to a more or less permanent take-over it is fairly evident that the country had reached a "stalemate" in the pursuit of modernization, as Coleman and Bryce suggested, it is impossible to determine by means of some objective measurements the critical level which "stalemate" must reach before military intervention is likely to take place. As I have suggested earlier, the countries in which they have occurred do not appear to be different as a group from those where they have not yet taken place. On the whole, however, it appears that the threshold of tolerance by the military of civilian regimes has been drastically lowered as the result of an increase in the frequency of successful military interventions elsewhere. If we now view the continent as an interacting system it is clear that a process of positive feedback is at work.

Events in the Sudan (1958, 1959), in the Congo (1960), and in Ethiopia (1960) do not seem to have had significant consequences for other countries, perhaps because none of these countries had been parts of larger colonial wholes, except for the relationship between the Congo, Rwanda, and Burundi. By contrast, a distinct wave of civilian and military coups, both successful and unsuccessful, swept former French Africa beginning in the second half of 1962 through January, 1964: the best-known coups occurred in Mali, Senegal, Ivory Coast, Togo, Congo-Brazzaville, Dahomey, Niger, and Gabon, in that order. They constituted a "wave" because they were perceived as such by the leaders who were all connected by traditions of political action within the framework of the former French Union and through common membership in inter-African organizations. Events in one country led to a shift from power to force in others, and to reactions by various groups often culminating in new plots and coups. On the other side of the continent, a similar wave occurred beginning in Zanzibar (January 12, 1964), and extending to Tanganyika (January 20), Uganda and Kenya (January 23). It is significant that in none of these cases did the military attempt to establish itself as a ruling elite.

The contrast with the wave of 1965 and 1966 is therefore very striking, since every military intervention during this period has been a take-over. Although it is very difficult to demonstrate that there were direct connections between events in Algeria (June, 1965), in the Congo (October), and the six other countries in which coups occurred between November, 1965, and February, 1966, there is no doubt that by this time African politicians as well as military officials were much more in touch with one another and with political life in the continent as a whole, through frequent meetings within the framework of international organizations inside and outside Africa and informal international activities.

For West Africa as a region, more direct links can be traced. As Philippe Decraene has indicated, Colonel Bokassa of the Central African Republic, Colonel Lamizana of Upper Volta, and General Soglo of Dahomey have known one another since they served together in Indochina.[20] Although it may be an exaggeration to speak as he does of a "freemasonry of veterans of Indochina," since there is no evidence of concerted action, it is likely that for each of these individuals the group as a whole constitutes a reference group similar to the one constituted by their predecessors who were alumni of William-Ponty.[21] The presence of one of these men at the helm of his country creates new status aspirations among the others. Another aspect of the phenomenon of contagion is suggested by General Soglo, who has explained that his take-over in Dahomey was prompted by the fear that the elections scheduled for early 1966 might crystallize the North-South cleavage and result in disorder similar to that which prevailed among the Yoruba of neighboring Western Nigeria during and after the electoral campaign of October, 1965, and about which Dahomeyans, many of whom are also Yoruba, were well informed.[22]

Conversely, Soglo's successful take-over probably affirmed the resolution of Nigerian officers next door. Their success, in turn, may have inspired their Ghanaian counterparts, with whom they share not only British professional traditions but also an exposure to the disastrous consequences of political disorder gained while serving with ONUC in the Congo.

Ultimately, however, the most important aspect of contagion and of escalation of military intervention from "referee action" to "take-over" is related to the changing definition of the situation: Coups seem to have occurred at first mainly in countries whose regimes were obviously weak; but the revelation of this prevalent weakness made even the more firmly established regimes much less formidable. It is as if a spell had been broken. The Army has now seen that the Emperor stands naked.

ASPECTS OF MILITARY RULE

Two questions must be raised about the new military regimes: First, are there any indications that the military elites are likely to innovate politically, both in the ideological and the structural sense? Second, how do the regimes they are creating look from the more general perspective of African political systems? Since no military regime has been in place for as much as one year at the time of writing, and since information available is still very scant, I cannot provide sound answers to these questions. Nevertheless, some possible trends can be suggested.

Although the behavior of the military rulers varies according to their own background, the situation at the time of the take-over, which contributed to these events, and the problems they are facing, there are striking similarities in the way in which they are approaching the problems of government and in the instrumentalities they are attempting to create to implement their goals.

In relation to the fundamental problem of political integration, conceived as the institutionalization of a formula for closing the elite–mass gap, military rulers think much like their predecessors in the one-party states.[23] They conceive of national unity as "oneness," defined negatively by the absence of social conflict stemming from regionalism, primordial loyalties such as ethnicity or religious affiliations. In all countries, "ethnic particularism" has been condemned and its manifestations through voluntary associations prohibited. The goal seems to be the achievement of homogeneity by political fiat, as if the rulers genuinely believed that the absence of conflict somehow *produces* national integration. Furthermore, integration means reinforcement of the tangible authority of the center. Regional autonomy and federal arrangements are viewed with suspicion as contributing factors, if not actual "causes," of malintegration. This trend has been manifested most clearly in the Congo-Kinshasa (formerly Leopoldville) and in the immediate postcoup period in Nigeria, where regional autonomy was greatest before the military take-over. In the Congo, General Mobutu has decreed that twenty-two provincial governments will be amalgamated into twelve; although these units will play an important role in political life, their role seems to be viewed as primarily administrative, following the continental model of the "prefect" system and its colonial equivalent. Although new elections have been held to choose officials at this level, General Mobutu has not hesitated to intervene when the outcome was considered to jeopardize the control by the center; military controllers supervise the operations of civilian executives and assemblies. Similarly, General Ironsi announced in May, 1966, that Nigeria would be ruled as a unitary state during the period of military government. The four major regions would be maintained temporarily as administrative units only, under direct military supervision, while the country was being broken up into undefined smaller units. Related to these changes were decisions to unify the Nigerian judiciary by reducing the autonomy of native courts, to merge the hitherto relatively autonomous civil services, and to create new central government ministries in the field of economics. (Since arrangements of this sort already prevailed in Ghana, Dahomey, the Central African Republic, and Upper Volta, it is important to note only that they are being maintained by the new rulers, except for some changes in detail and personnel.)

Thus the Nigerian military leaders acted in much the same manner as military rulers elsewhere. It was only after the Nigerian military itself ceased to exist as a national entity that a bias for centralization was no longer evident; both Northern and Eastern Nigerian officers were committed to strong central rule when they were in command. It is likely that they will act within their regions, or separate states if Nigeria should dissolve entirely, in a manner that is little different from their colleagues in other countries.

Military rulers apply much the same reasoning toward political competition and have generally banned political parties. It is significant that in most cases this ban has not been limited to organizations that were in power at the time of the take-over, but has even been extended to include those which were then in opposition, and whose critiques of the former regimes were similar to those voiced by the military itself. In Ghana, for example, K. Busia was allowed to return home from exile, went on a "lecture" tour, but left soon afterwards, allegedly at the request of General Ankrah. Although southerners, and particularly Ironsi, were prominent in the Nigerian military coup, it is significant that they did not call upon President Azikiwe to take the helm, but merely allowed him to return to Nigeria as a "private citizen"; southern opposition leaders such as Chief Awolowo and Chief Enahoro for a time remained under detention where they had been placed by the previous regime. General Soglo initially appeared to be negotiating with the usual Dahomeyan triumvirate—Maga, Apithy, and Ahomadegbe—but within a few months they had all left the country for Paris. Similarly, although Colonel Bokassa initially made a point of stressing his loyalty to the ruling party, Mouvement d'Evolution Sociale en Afrique Noire (MESAN), founded by his deceased uncle, Barthelemy Boganda, and of appearing in public with his deposed cousin, former President David Dacko, insisting that the coup had not been directed at Dacko personally but rather at his evil associates, he later indicated that the military would rule directly "by popular request" and that all political activity would be suspended. Although President Yameogo of Upper Volta declared that he welcomed the military take-over, this does not appear to have earned him a place in the new sun; there are no indications that the situation differs significantly there from the other countries considered. General Mobutu announced very early that "the race for the summit is over; the deposed politicians are free to do what they want," except presumably to interfere with the new order, but did not take immediate action to suspend all political activity. More recently, however, some of the best-known politicians seem to be departing from the scene: Lumumbist Antoine Gizenga was released from detention, took his place in Parliament, but later fled the country; Moise Tshombe is also in exile; Cyrille Adoula has been "promoted" Ambassador to Belgium; Evariste Kimba was executed with several minor figures for participation in an anti-Mobutu plot; Cleophas Kamitatu has been arrested; and although former President Kasavubu (whom the Army supported against Lumumba in 1960) is free, some observers believe that the Army is slowly moving against him by eliminating his supporters.[24]

The suspension of conflict has been extended to include economic bargaining by occupational groups. In Dahomey, where the Army had once intervened on behalf of trade unionists, the military rulers have warned that there is to be no more bargaining: as one of the leaders put it, if civil servants want higher salaries, let them take over the government. The military governments of Upper Volta and of the Central African Republic have granted to the civil servants' trade unions some of the demands they had been making at the time of the take-over, but then also warned them that they must refrain from formulating further ones and have taken measures to restrict the freedom of association. General Mobutu abruptly ended a teachers' strike and seized the opportunity to prohibit all strikes. Although the National Liberation Committee of Ghana has promised that the trade unions would never again be transformed into quasi-official bodies, it remains to be seen how it will react to the onerous demands for economic reallocations that African unions are prone to make at regular intervals.

Although each of the military ruling groups has indicated in turn that the suspension of political activity is temporary, they all appear to be settling down to the regular business of government, moving from a sort of collegial emergency "revolutionary" council to a more normal form of cabinet organization. Usually, one or more senior military figures are at the helm, either as President, or as Chairman of the Council, or in the form of a two-headed executive (President and Prime Minister). The composition of their cabinets, usually akin to advisory executive councils, varies somewhat from case to case. In every country the military rules have retained direct control over the military itself (Ministry of Defense), over the police (Ministry of the Interior), and often over finances. The remainder usually consists of lesser officers and "technocrats," established senior civil servants or newcomers, usually educated men with high professional qualifications but with little or no administrative experience, and a sprinkling of politicians "above reproach." In Ghana the police, which participated in the coup, shares with the Army all eight cabinet posts; although most senior civil servants had been highly critical of the deposed regime, they seem to be used in an advisory capacity only. The Congo deviates somewhat from the pattern in that besides Army control of the Presidency and the office of Prime Minister, the cabinet has been established on the basis of regional representation and includes a number of politicians.

Representative bodies have been suspended or dissolved, or their authority has been severely curtailed. The Army is accountable to itself alone, in the name of the nation, but tends to consult various ad hoc bodies as the occasion arises. Although General Mobutu initially submitted his decisions to Parliament for approval, he later announced that his decrees would have force of law unless they are specifically reversed by Parliament; finally, after five months in office, expressing his disappointment at the behavior of the lower house, he reduced it to the status of a consultative body only for the duration of his tenure of office. The unicameral National Assembly of Dahomey has been replaced by a 35-man "National Renovation Committee" whose authority is not clear; the National Assemblies of the Central African Republic and of Upper Volta have been dissolved, along with municipal council and regional bodies, as has the Ghanaian National Assembly. There is some talk everywhere of creating consultative committees, some of which may be empowered to draft constitutional proposals, but the criteria for selection of their members and the degree of freedom they will have cannot yet be discerned.

It is equally difficult to determine whether or not, or to what extent, African armies intend to become involved in the direct management of specialized administrative agencies, in territorial administration, and in the creation of new aggregative structures akin to political parties. Most of them seem to have limited themselves to the appointment of military governors to head major territorial divisions such as departments, provinces, regions, or districts, or to the designation of military supervisors over civil servants who continue to man specialized administrative agencies. African armies usually have little choice in this respect, since they seldom have sufficient cadres of their own to attempt more direct control over management. Some effort to achieve the latter goal is apparent in Dahomey, however, where the new Commander-in-Chief has sought French assistance for the creation of a highly mobile unit of airborne commandos in order to free the remainder of the Army for more active participation in administration, on the grounds that it alone possesses the discipline which is needed in this sphere. Much in the same vein, the Congolese government has given some publicity to a report prepared by Lovanium University which states that the country's administration is so unwieldy that a total renovation under direct military management may well be necessary.

On the whole, relations between the military and civil servants seem to be good; yet it is also clear that the Army will exercise close supervision over government employees, and that good feelings will last only so long as the latter behave according to Army standards. The repeated decision by several regional governors in Nigeria, upon inspecting government offices after the start of the working day, to dispatch their troops to round up all latecomers, may bring about a temporary spurt of efficiency but is unlikely to reinforce the Army-civil service governing alliance most of the regimes are apparently attempting to build as a substitute for politics. Only in the Congo, where General Mobutu has spoken of the creation of a nation-wide "Council of Youth" which would absorb all existing "youth wings," is there some indication that military rulers are giving some thought to the engineering of structures that can transform directives from the center into genuine political communications and secure information from the country-at-large without which no regime can long maintain itself, except by dealing forcibly with all demands.[25]

It is not surprising that all the military rulers are acting swiftly to secure a genuine monopoly over the instruments of force in their respective countries. In most cases, this has merely required the dissolution of special bodies such as Presidential guards and party militias, or the reintegration of their cadres into the regular Army. Elsewhere, however, it has necessitated the establishment of tight military controls over the gendarmerie and the police force, as well as the purge of unreliable personnel within the Army's own ranks. Although Nigeria may have been on the brink of a general flare-up in the South at the time of the take-over, only the Congo was in the throes of an internal war. There, the Army seems to have continued to gain over the rebel organizations, which had already shown signs of internal dissension and complete exhaustion before the take-over. The government's position appears to be a willingness to grant amnesty to individuals, but a refusal to negotiate with their leaders. It was announced in June, 1966, that Pierre Mulele had laid down his arms. The Mobutu government has also taken steps to remove the notorious European and white South African "mercenaries" from the Army.

It is more difficult to discover common patterns in the field of foreign policy, where variations among countries were initially greatest. Nevertheless, the different actions of the military rulers, taken where applicable, seem to be leading toward a generalized "moderate" position on international issues most relevant to Africa, disengagement from involvement in more irrelevant issues, and the maintenance or reinforcement of symbols of national sovereignty. With respect to relations with the former colonial power, there has been little change in Upper Volta, the Central African Republic, or Dahomey, but there has been a rapprochement between Ghana and Great Britain, on the one hand, and a reassertion of Congolese independence from Belgium, on the other, signaled by the renaming of major cities and by a fairly tough position on the negotiation of various outstanding economic issues. While remaining "neutralist," the military rulers seem less "militant" than some of their predecessors. The only significant change here is the generalized distrust of Communist Chinese penetration, as well as the ending of some far-fetched Eastern European schemes in Ghana. The new governments also appear to be making a genuine effort to bring about a detente in inter-African relations. The most dramatic change in this respect, as in the entire field of foreign policy, has occurred in Ghana, whose new rulers have been actively engaged in settling disputes with their neighbors. This trend may be a prelude to the reinforcement of functional cooperation on a regional or continental scale; at the same time, however, it is unlikely that the military governments will show much interest in large-scale pan-Africanist schemes.

Whatever the stimuli that prompted the military to intervene in recent years, they have always included a belief that their countries have deviated from the straight and narrow path which leads to modernity. Hence, it is through an examination of the ideological maps the new rulers are using to plan their campaign that we can best understand the constraints upon their own behavior and the measures they are likely to take to guide their countrymen. From this point of view, the most important public activity in which they have engaged so far has been the investigation of "corruption." The most prominent aspect of their style of leadership is a display of barracks-room austerity, reflected across the board by the drastic curtailment of the salaries of high officials, but perhaps best symbolized by General Soglo's decision to turn off the palace air-conditioners in Cotonou. The economic plans they have inherited are being revised to eliminate some of their most unworkable features, such as the plethora of state enterprises in Ghana, but the concept of planning itself remains fundamental. The military rulers share with their predecessors a fundamental faith in the ability of men to overcome underdevelopment by means of rational behavior and detailed economic, social, and political engineering.[26] Failure to modernize rapidly, then, is not thought to be the result of the inherent difficulties of the program itself in relation to the society on which it is imposed, but rather of selfishness, laziness, and corruption. Hence, government must be entrusted only to men who are capable of self-control, honesty, and hard work. Where, except among soldiers, will individuals with such qualities be found?

CONCLUSIONS

WHAT can we make of these tentative patterns? Returning to the question of "innovation," it appears that with respect to general constitutional arrangements, the greatest change is occurring in Nigeria and in the Congo, the two countries which deviated most from what had earlier become the model African regime. In the sphere of economic and foreign policy, however, Ghana, the country which among those under consideration deviated most from a model position, is undergoing the greatest change. Hence, we can tentatively conclude that despite some innovation within any given country, there is little or no innovation in the group as a whole. If military rulers reach what appear to be their present goals, it is likely that these countries will tend ultimately to become more alike in terms of their regimes and economic orientations, and also more like those in which civilian modernizing oligarchies survive.

Faced with the problems of government in poorly integrated, heterogeneous societies, military oligarchies in Africa are attempting to create a form of the "administrative state" which resembles in many respects the colonial regimes during their terminal phase of "welfare colonialism." The paradox is that many of the regimes against which military intervention was originally directed also resembled their colonial predecessors. Everywhere, the concern with political order, administrative efficiency, and rational economic planning has led African rulers to reduce the effects of the rapid expansion of political participation during the period of decolonization and nationalism.

In the light of the politicians' inability to maintain themselves in office and of the lurid headlines revealing their corruption and incompetence, it is easy to forget that they had initially been relatively successful in developing symbols and organizations which could be used to channel support and to establish the legitimacy of their claim to rule in the eyes of their countrymen. Is it likely that the military rulers will show equal or greater skill in creating a political formula which can begin to bridge the gap between the elite and the masses? It is much too early to be able to detect the results of their efforts in this respect because the military oligarchies initially benefit from the great sense of relief with which the downfall of their predecessors was greeted.

Although the General-Presidents, the Major-Ministers, or Captain-Governors seem to be honest, hard-working, and even considerate of their fellow-countrymen's civil liberties, they are faced with the same society as the one which led to the rapid deterioration of party solidarity, bureaucratic responsibility, and rule of law so soon after the new states were born amidst general enthusiasm and hope. The institutionalization of constitutional government based on legitimacy and political power rather than force requires the internalization by the elite at the top and in the middle, as well as by an important proportion of the participant masses, of a complex set of norms which are not yet widespread in Africa. Hence, much as even the apparently best-organized party-states came to reflect the society which produced them as they attempted to extend their control over the society, so military-sponsored regimes will come to reflect this society. Although on the surface, and from the point of view of current events, the wave of military coups in Africa appears to signify a major change in the continent's political complexion, from the point of view of political modernization these events probably constitute merely an interesting episode in a protracted struggle. This confirms the notion that state-building necessarily precedes nation-building; that the state, in Africa, does not encompass the political system as a whole; and that under these conditions, force will continue to be a prominent aspect of the political process.

From this point of view, the most remarkable aspect of military coups in Africa remains the ease with which established regimes were dissolved and the initial absence of popular reaction to these events beyond some manifestations of joy in a few urban centers. To dismiss this by arguing that the outgoing regimes were almost unanimously unpopular somehow misses the point because in every country many individuals and groups did thrive under these regimes and appeared to have a great deal to lose by their disappearance. Furthermore, although military take-overs were often preceded by popular unrest, as we have seen in our discussion of the circumstances of their origins, this unrest was never sufficiently generalized to hamper the survival of regimes *until* the military intervened. When this occurred, even the incumbent leaders (where they survived) bowed to the show of force. In many countries, the ousted politicians are vying with one another to dissociate themselves from the old regime and to pledge allegiance to the new, much as a few years earlier many of them had jumped on the bandwagon of the dominant party.

This suggests a puzzling aspect of politics in many parts of Africa: a tendency to accept whatever authority establishes a claim to rule on the basis of force, as if force generates its own legitimacy. This authority is then generally accepted until it demonstrates in one way or another that it has lost the substance of its initial force, usually when a new champion arises. The population is seldom involved in the drama itself but stands on the sidelines, as if watching a joust, choosing contestants but rapidly shifting its allegiance to the winner. Whether this phenomenon is genuine, whether it is rooted in some ill-understood feature of African cultures, perpetuated by some important aspects of the process of socialization and personality formation, whether it can be accounted for in situational and structural terms, or even how this puzzle can be transformed into a researchable problem, are questions beyond my reach at the present time and outside the bounds of this study. But they remind us once again that comparative research in Africa as elsewhere must be firmly rooted in an understanding of the unique qualities of societies.

NOTES

1. The designation "new states of tropical Africa" includes all countries south of the Sahara and north of the Zambezi, except Liberia and Ethiopia.

2. Coleman, James S., and Belmont Bryce, Jr., "The Role of the Military in Sub-Saharan Africa," in Johnson, John J., editor, *The Role of the Military in Underdeveloped Countries.* Princeton University Press, Princeton, N.J., 1962, pp. 359–405.

3. *Ibid.,* p. 399.

4. *Ibid.,* p. 402.

5. The most useful surveys of African military establishments are contained in the publications of the Institute of Strategic Studies (London). See in particular Bell, M. J. V., "Army and Nation in Sub-Saharan Africa," *Adelphi Papers* No. 21, August, 1965; and Wood, David, "The Armed Forces of African States," *Adelphi Papers* No. 27, April, 1966.

6. This discussion of "society" owes a great deal to the discussion in Smith, M. G., *The Plural Society in the British West Indies,* University of California Press, Berkeley and Los Angeles, 1965, pp. 65–91.

7. For this use of "political system," see the works of David Easton, particularly *A Framework for Political Analysis,* Prentice-Hall, Englewood Cliffs, N.J., 1965.

8. More positive evidence requires the accumulation of micropolitical studies, such as the studies of Ghana reported by David Brokensha and Ernst Benjamin at the October, 1965, meetings of the African Studies Association in Philadelphia. Nicholas Hopkins is currently completing a study of this type on Mali.

9. See in particular the introduction and conclusions of James S. Coleman and Carl S. Rosberg, Jr., editors, *Political Parties and National Integration in Tropical Africa,* University of California Press, Berkelely and Los Angeles, 1965; and Apter, David, *The Politics of Modernization,* University of Chicago Press, Chicago, 1965.

10. Undoubtedly, countries of this type are simply less attractive to social scientists than "mass party" countries. For a discussion of their political organizations, see in particular the concept of "patron" or "cadre" party in Hodgkin, Thomas, *African Political Parties*, Penguin Books, Baltimore, 1961, and Schachter [Morgenthau], Ruth, "Single-Party Systems in West Africa," *American Political Science Review*, vol. 55, no. 2, June, 1961, pp. 294–312.

11. See especially Berg, Elliot, and Jeffrey Butler, "Trade Unions," in Coleman, James S., and Carl S. Rosberg, Jr., editors, *op. cit.*, pp. 340–381.

12. Parsons, Talcott, "Some Reflections on the Place of Force in Social Process," in Eckstein, Harry, editor, *Internal War*. The Free Press of Glencoe, New York, 1964, p. 59.

13. *Ibid.*, p. 60.

14. *Ibid.*, p. 64.

15. *Ibid.*, p. 66.

16. This seems to have been the case most clearly in Ghana and in the Central African Republic, as well as in the abortive 1966 coup in the Congo-Brazzaville.

17. The events of December, 1962, in Senegal, which involved a sparring contest between the gendarerie and airborne troops, are summarized in DuBois, Victor D., "The Trial of Mamadou Dia," *American Universities Field Staff, Report Service*, West Africa Series, vol. 6, no. 6, June, 1963, pp. 4–8.

18. See the analysis of Dahomey and Congo-Brazzaville in Terray, Emmanuel, "Les révolutions congolaise et dahoméene de 1963: essai d'interpretation," *Revue Française de Science Politique*, vol. 14, no. 5, October, 1964, pp. 917–942.

19. For a review of relations between the military and the Nkrumah regime and an analysis of the coup, see Kraus, Jon, "The Men in Charge," *Africa Report*, vol. 11, no. 4, April, 1966, pp. 16–20.

20. *Le Monde, Sélection Hebdomadaire*, June 30–July 6, 1966.

21. William-Ponty, a normal school in Senegal, was the apex of the educational pyramid for French Africans who were not "citizens" before World War II. It produced teachers, physicians, and middle-level clerks, many of whom went on to lead parties and to staff cabinets.

22. Reported by P. Decraene in *Le Monde, loc. cit.*

23. The concept of "political integration" as used here is based on the exposition by Leonard Binder in "National Integration and Political Development," *American Political Science Review*, vol. 58, no. 3, September, 1964, pp. 622–631.

24. This interpretation is offered by "Griot" in *West Africa*, June 11, 1966.

25. Normally, an organization of this sort in Africa would be headed by a High Commissioner for Youth and Sports, a post filled initially by Antoine Gizenga after his release. It is not clear whether that was in fact the

government's intention, or whether plans have been changed since Gizenga left the country.

26. For an early analysis of the prevalence of this faith, see Sutton, Francis X., "Planning and Rationality in the Newly Independent States in Africa," *Economic Development and Cultural Change,* vol. 10, 1961, pp. 42–50. I have developed the implications of this type of ideology in *Creating Political Order: The Party-States of West Africa,* Rand McNally and Co., Chicago, 1966, chap. 2.

After the Seizure of Power:
The Struggle for Stability

PART TWO

After the Seizure of Power:
The Struggle for Stability

IT IS difficult to draw a firm dividing line between the initial phase of military involvement and this second phase, the struggle for stability. In a sense, the second phase begins the day the military takes power. We might allow time to determine whether the military is going to hand back power to some civilian group right away (the first Burmese intervention of the Army; the first Dahomeyan intervention; Togo; Burundi for a few weeks before the Army intervened again.)

South Korea, South Vietnam, and Burma are among the countries where the military has taken over and continues to rule and struggle to bring about acceptance of its rule as well as development. Although there have been changes in leadership, there has been a large carry-over from the original group who conducted the initial take-overs. This is true for both the United Arab Republic and Pakistan, although the generals who led the coups in name have been replaced. In the UAR and Pakistan there seems less challenge to military rule than in Korea. However, both might be placed in this category because of the absence of numbers of coups and counter-coups. The struggle in Pakistan and the UAR, however, might be better termed one for development than for immediate stability, since the military regimes seem more fully in command than in Korea. It would also be appropriate to consider Indonesia here as the military regime tries to solidify its position in a situation of competing political groups.

The criteria for inclusion in this category are: (1) a regime dominated by the military; (2) a military which has a great deal of continuity with the original leaders of the coup; (3) a situation which has not been characterized by a number of military involvements. Thus, we are dealing with a first generation of military leaders. Examining the countries in this category, we want to know how the military tries to build political support for itself and how it succeeds or fails as a modernizer.

Sohn shows how the Korean military has reached out for a political base and how it has lost its position "above politics" in the process. He also casts doubt on the military as the nation-builder. In order to test his propositions about Korea against other situations, we need similar studies of Burma, Pakistan, and the UAR. For example, Sohn notes that a high proportion of the South Korean national budget goes to military expenditures. Certain civilian regimes show a similar phenomenon either because their defense needs are perceived to be great (the USSR and the United States) or because the military is an effective pressure group on civilian government (Iran, Ethiopia, Afghanistan).[1] Obviously, both factors may be present at once. Thus, a high rate of expenditure on military forces is not ipso facto a consequence of military rule. However, regimes run by the military do not on the whole show relatively low rates of expenditure on military forces. While it is conceivable that a military government could hold defense expenditures down, even with more efficacy than a civilian government, our evidence from statistical correlations shows this is unlikely. Nonetheless, it is necessary to demonstrate the breakdown of defense expenditures (hardware, salaries, retirement benefits, and so on) and to see who may restrain the military and how. We need studies describing the ways in which the military government determines its allocations and to what pressures it responds as it takes on the task of rule and acts as a political group.

NOTE

1. See Janowitz, Morris, *The Military in the Political Development of New Nations,* University of Chicago Press, Chicago, 1964, pp. 20–21, Table 2, Basic Data on Armed Forces of New Nations.

Political Dominance and Political Failure:
The Role of the Military in the Republic of Korea*
by Jae Souk Sohn

In the Republic of Korea, as in many other new states in Asia and Africa, the military has played an important political role in the past few years. On May 16, 1961, a Korean military group assumed political control of the government after a period of ineffective civilian parliamentary leadership, climaxed by a crisis precipitated by a series of antigovernment demonstrations. In December, 1963, the military junta formally transferred political power to a civilian government chosen in national elections. But the actual control of the government remained in the hands of the junta's core members, who had entered domestic politics as "civilians" against their original revolutionary pledges. General Chung Hee Park, Chief of the Military Junta, became President and head of the new civilian government for a four-year term, and his Democratic-Republican Party, which had been created during the military rule, secured an absolute majority in the National Assembly. Furthermore, since the military coup, many military officers have been converted into high-ranking government officials, diplomats, and top managers of public corporations. Thus, the military has emerged as a crucial institution and power bloc, setting the style of Korean politics in a new direction. This study will examine the causes of the 1961 military coup from the viewpoint of the internal social organization of the military, trace the changing pattern of civilian-military relations, and evaluate the role of the military in Korea's modernization process.

INTERNAL SOCIAL ORGANIZATION OF THE MILITARY

The South Korean Armed Forces were first built up after liberation from Imperial Japan in 1945. During the thirty-six years of Japanese

---

* This is a paper presented to the working group on "Militarism and the Professional Military Man" of the Sixth World Congress of the International Sociological Association, Evian, France, September 4–10, 1966.

colonial rule, Korea's indigenous military institution had been eliminated and displaced by the metropolitan power. The Japanese exercised direct rule in order to assimilate the Korean territory into their imperial system. As a first step in the process of occupying Korea, the Japanese imposed a protectorate status in 1905; and two years later, they disbanded the Royal Army of the old Korean kingdom. In the long period beginning with formal annexation in 1910, Japanese rule rested on a form of military government; as a result, the military profession was not open to the indigenous people. After the Japanese seizure of Manchuria in 1931, however, this policy was modified. The Japanese trained a limited number of Korean officers for service in the Japanese Armed Forces as well as the Japanese-controlled Manchurian Army, although they drafted hundreds of thousands of Korean youths during the protracted Sino-Japanese War and World War II. As a result, the withdrawal of Japanese colonial rule from Korea left behind no self-contained native army.

Immediately after national liberation in August, 1945, several private military or paramilitary organizations were formed, with the common objective of building up a unitary national army.[1] These organizations were quickly dissolved when the American military government in South Korea took steps to create a small-scale Korean constabulary as its subsidiary organ for the area's internal order and external defense. Toward the end of 1945 the American military government set up a Military English School, predecessor of the Korean Military Academy, which was designed to train a professional cadre of the prospective Korean military establishment. When the South Korean constabulary came into being in January, 1946, it had as officers some one hundred graduates of this school, who had received training by the American military for a few weeks. Since the constabulary officer corps was made up almost entirely of personnel who had served under the Japanese, the Manchurians, or the Chinese, the different military backgrounds of corps members had a significant impact upon the new Korean military institution. Apart from being poorly armed, the South Korean constabulary, which was steadily expanded during the period of American rule, was heterogeneous in terms of personnel, organization, and training.

This rudimentary military establishment was transformed into the regular South Korean Armed Forces in August, 1948, when the Republic of Korea proclaimed its independence. The withdrawal of the

American Occupation Forces from South Korea was accompanied by positive measures to develop rapidly the three services of the Korean Armed Forces. But until the outbreak of the Korean War in June, 1950, the national army was still a fragile structure composed of fewer than 100,000 men, whose functions were directed to the suppression of communist insurrections in the rear, as well as to the defense of the 38th parallel. During the Korean War, the Korean Army was built up as the world's fourth largest anticommunist force of nearly one million men with massive American military aid. After the armistice of July, 1953, the total manpower of the Korean Armed Forces was gradually reduced until by 1960 it reached its present level of 600,000. Since they were established, the Armed Forces of the Republic of Korea have been heavily dependent upon American support for their maintenance and development.

In the midst of profound internal difficulties and continued external threats following the division of the Korean peninsula, the national army had a central place in the Republic, born as an anticommunist frontier country. From the first year of independence the constant problem of communist subversion forced the Army to assume direct responsibilities for law and order in many districts, and during the Korean War, Army authority was expanded to cover the entire country. After the cease-fire some military men in the top echelons were frequently involved in domestic politics for personal gain. As a matter of fact, the Korean military had been a vital factor in the complex of political power even during the years preceding the military coup of 1961.

However, the military had been an instrument rather than a master of the civilian government, largely because of the skill with which the Liberal Party government, and particularly President Syngman Rhee, had handled military leaders. By his authoritarian, personal control, the founding father was able to use the military to throttle political opposition and to manipulate elections. But after the Rhee regime fell in the student uprising of April 19, 1960, the newly elected Democratic Party cabinet headed by John M. Chang was too weak to maintain civilian supremacy over the military, which had been accustomed to a strong personal control. As a result, after less than one year in power, the ineffective parliamentary government was overthrown by the military.

In the coup of May 16, 1961, a group of military officers seized power when a stalemate developed in the struggle between two competing factions in the ruling Democratic Party. To justify their action, they maintained that they were forced to take over by the failure of civilian government, and that they came to power with the purest of patriotic intentions to save the country from chaos, corruption, and communism. Although power went by default to the military officers, a number of considerations suggest that most of their drive for power came from the progressive crumbling of the military order since the armistice of the Korean War.

In Korea, the military profession suffers in social esteem largely because of Confucian tradition; therefore, the military officers have been recruited from middle and lower classes and from rural areas (Table 1). In its formative period before the Korean War, the mili-

Table 1

FATHER'S OCCUPATION OF OFFICERS GRADUATED
FROM MILITARY ACADEMY IN FOUR-YEAR
CADET COURSE, 1955–1962

Occupation	Per cent
Farmer	31
Small business	29
White-collar	20
Professional	6
Military officer	4
Other	10
Total	100
Number of cases	*1,386*

SOURCE: Computed from personal data filed at the Korean Military Academy for first class (1955) through eighth class (1962).

tary attracted young men from humble families who had little formal education but were seeking an avenue of upward social mobility. The military was accessible to these young men, and their social position and educational background did not hinder their success in their careers. The three years of the Korean War had made the Armed Forces more important as the bulwarks of the state, had required larger defense budgets, and had broadened internal functions of the military. Consequently, the prestige of the military as a profession had risen considerably and, in fact, the officer corps had become the most favored group in the country. In the postwar years, however, their relatively high prestige and advantageous status were declining, while the civilian politicians frequently interfered in the internal affairs of the Armed Forces and tried to use them for their own purposes. In addition, the professional officers were threatened by the problem of demobilization which had been posed since the armistice of 1953. Thus, the frustration and decline in power of the officer corps as a dominant group contributed to their readiness to assume political power.

Since a purge of leftist dissidents from the Army in 1948–1949, the Korean military has been a relatively integrated combat organization based on American-modeled training and anticommunist combat experience. But significant internal cleavages have complicated its political intervention. One source of cleavage was the existence of various informal groups or factions based on foreign military background, influential personality, regional origin, Military Academy class, and so on. Since the early years of the Korean Army, factionalism had been an important factor in the practice of patronage regarding promotion and assignment, so that unfair personnel management weakened discipline in the officer corps. At crucial moments of internal military politics, there occurred struggles among the three groups of foreign-trained senior officers; between two powerful groups of middle-rank officers— graduates of the fifth class and those of the eighth class of the old Korean Military Academy, which provided a crash program of one- to six-month career training in 1946–1950. As in civilian society and government, the North Korean minority, who actually dominated the Army throughout the whole precoup period, have maintained the most cohesive group to remain in an advantageous position to promote their interests. After the officers of South Korean origin came to dominate the military government, the North Korean minority repeatedly sought to launch counter-coups.

A more serious source of tension in the Korean military was conflict between the generals and the colonels in the aftermath of the April, 1960, student revolution. The political and social turmoil after the student revolution affected the military, and the dramatic struggle that occurred between the old and the new and between the partisans of the traditional order and the supporters of the emerging forces in civilian society was clearly mirrored in the officer corps. In the midst of growing military disorder, young colonels initiated a "reorganization movement" for the Army, which was destined to become a major political issue for the period of Chang's government. The movement called for the discharge of corrupt, politically compromised generals to secure rapid promotions for the junior officers. In September, 1960, a group of sixteen Army colonels armed with pistols, mostly drawn from the eighth Academy class, broke in upon Lt. General Yung Hee Choi, Chairman of the Joint Chiefs of Staff, and forced him to resign, telling him: "You are a lucky guy, General! You have now become Chairman of the Joint Chiefs of Staff through Division Commander, Corps Commander, Field Army Commander, and Army Chief of Staff. Like other generals, why don't you move out to a better post, such as Minister of Defense or Foreign Ambassador, and thereby open up the way for the newcomers?"[2] Less than one year after this revolt took place, the colonel group led a successful military coup under the direction of Major General Chung Hee Park.[3]

This cleavage resulted from a serious "promotional freeze" which began to emerge after the armistice of the Korean War. As described earlier, the Korean military was created anew in 1945 and thereafter expanded rapidly in a short period of time. Hence the officer corps, particularly of the formative period 1946–1950, was filled with men of roughly the same age, but they had unparalleled opportunities for promotion. Those first on the scene were catapulted into the rank of general in their twenties or early thirties and the later arrivals filled the junior ranks (Table 2). Furthermore, since all high posts in the military echelons had been occupied by young generals, the opportunity of promotion for lower-ranking officers decreased continuously as postwar demobilization proceeded. This introduced serious promotional problems and increased the possibility of frustration and intrigue in the junior ranks.

The young colonels with less seniority had fewer vested interests in the military status quo. And they were less committed to the social and political status quo and were more involved in contemporary political currents. Thus, they were inclined toward a more radical outlook.[4] On the other hand, the long absence of war since the armistice had left them with time to pursue extramilitary activities, including political ones. Probably recent developments abroad, such as a series of successful military coups in Burma, Pakistan, and Turkey, encouraged their determination to take over.[5] On May 16, 1961, they finally rode to power at the head of popular reform movements then active among student circles.

It is true that the military take-over was precipitated by the corruption and incompetence of the civilian government. Basically, however,

Table 2

PROMOTION RATE OF OFFICERS, 1946–1962

Military English Class (1946, one-month training)

Years	2nd Lt. Major	Lt. Colonel	Colonel	Brigadier General	Maj. General	Lt. General	General
	PERCENTAGES						
1	19	8	1	—	—	—	—
2	76	24	6	—	—	—	—
3	3	64	12	2	—	—	—
4	2	4	77	44	9	—	—
5	—	—	3	12	7	8	—
6	—	—	1	11	20	12	—
7	—	—	—	21	22	8	25
8	—	—	—	6	6	20	50
9	—	—	—	4	9	20	—
10	—	—	—	—	—	4	—
11	—	—	—	—	4	—	—
12	—	—	—	—	6	—	—
13	—	—	—	—	11	—	—
14	—	—	—	—	—	8	—
15	—	—	—	—	6	20	—
16	—	—	—	—	—	—	25
Total	100	100	100	100	100	100	100
Number of cases	*91*	*85*	*77*	*72*	*54*	*25*	*4*

Eighth Academy Class (1949, four- to six-month training)

Years	2nd Lt. 1st Lt.	Captain	Major	Lt. Colonel	Colonel
	PERCENTAGES				
1	91.6	—	—	—	—
2	8.2	97.2	4.5	—	—
3	0.1	2.6	—	—	—
4	0.1	—	80.5	2.6	—
5	—	0.1	7.0	1.8	—
6	—	—	6.8	47.0	—
7	—	0.1	0.8	29.6	—
8	—	—	—	8.9	4.8
9	—	—	0.1	7.8	—
10	—	—	0.3	2.2	4.8
11	—	—	—	0.1	8.3
12	—	—	—	—	78.6
13	—	—	—	—	3.5
Total	100	100	100	100	100
Number of cases	*1,207*	*898*	*763*	*683*	*145*

First Cadet Class (1955, four-year training)

Years	2nd Lt.	1st Lt.	Captain	Major
	PERCENTAGES			
1	—		—	—
2	99		—	—
3	1		—	—
4	—		—	—
5	—		99	—
6	—		1	—
7	—		—	100
Total	100		100	100
Number of cases	*155*		*151*	*43*

SOURCE: Lee, In Keun, "A Study of the Officers' Promotion System," unpublished MPA thesis, Seoul National University, Seoul, Korea, 1962, pp. 66, 104–113.

the Korean military coup was the consequence of an equal corruption and internal disorder of the military organization as well as the reaction of a power group—that is, the military—which had been expanded as a result of United States Far East policy against communism, to another group—the civilian politicians—who had been trying to control such a large standing military force.

CHANGING PATTERNS OF CIVILIAN-MILITARY RELATIONS

THE military coup of May, 1961, brought to power the Supreme Council of National Reconstruction (SCNR), composed of some thirty coup officers, including top military commanders. When the military officers first took over, they promised a speedy return to civilian government after they carried out a revolutionary task for political change, economic development, and social reformation. In addition to the usual procedure of blacklisting traditional and corrupt politicians, the military junta proceeded with radical and comprehensive measures. And yet, as will be examined later, it was unsuccessful in carrying out the revolutionary task for various reasons, the most important of which was the inherent limitations of military officers for political affairs, coupled with a fierce power struggle within the ruling junta.

The striking aspect of the Korean military junta was that it sought to conserve its political influence, in whatever form, after a return to civilian rule. As a result, in early 1962 the core members of the military junta, who had determined to participate in civilian politics, took clandestine steps to organize a mass political party by dipping into the national treasury.[6] After permitting civilian political activity as of January 1, 1963, and declaring elections for the restoration of civilian rule to be held in late 1963, they resigned from active duty to become the cadre of this new party, named the Democratic-Republican Party (DRP). Meanwhile, the military junta managed to effect a constitutional change on a popular vote, which was intended to establish a system for strong government—that is, a presidential form of government with a unicameral legislature. Therefore, it was not surprising when General Chung Hee Park, Chairman of the SCNR, decided that, by dishonoring his original promise, he would run for the October, 1963, presidential election as a "civilian" under the sponsorship of the military-created political party. Such a prearranged program worked well enough to transform the military junta itself into a new civilian government, for General Park assumed a four-year term presidency strengthened with solid support of an almost two-thirds majority from his DRP in the concurrent National Assembly.[7]

The majority of the military junta opposed any civilian party government as likely to deteriorate the political situation after the transfer of power. In fact, they feared it might negate the validity of the "military revolution" and retaliate against them. However, the "designed" transfer of power to the new military-dominated civilian government in December, 1963, through elections, did not create political stability. The internal political life of Korea has since been beset by conflicts between political parties and frequent and intensive student demonstrations against government.

When we look into the character of Park's DRP regime, we find that it is a military-civilian coalition, but with hegemony in the hands of military-become-civilian politicians in both the party and the government. Since, in the process of transferring power, they recognized the needs for a mass political base, they have developed this system of alliance with old politicians, a considerable number of whom have been recruited from the former Liberal Party of Syngman Rhee. Although on the surface it appears to be a relatively stable coalition, it should be noted that tensions are bound to exist between former military officers and their civilian partners. The influx of retired officers into key posts in the bureaucracy since the military coup has aroused a particular sense of insecurity among civilian officials and has disturbed the discipline of the civil service. New appointments in the government and public corporations tend to be made for the particular interests of the military class rather than on the basis of achievements and competence.

The political dominance of former military men, combined with unceasing reliance on police and espionage methods and with increasing corruption in the government, seems to be the fundamental cause of the civilian resistance which has continued since the restoration of constitutional rule. In general, the conflict is between the ruling party and the opposition—between the government, on the one hand, and students, intellectuals, and journalists, on the other. Such confrontations have been intensified by outright disagreement on major foreign policy issues, such as the normalization of Korean-Japanese relations and the dispatch of Korean troops to South Vietnam. The basic attitude of opposition parties can be found in the condemnation of the DRP regime as an extension of military rule dressed in constitutional garb. University student groups are centers of opposition, too. The government regards these opposition forces as irresponsible and almost traitorous and meets them with repressive measures. Thus, Korean politics operates in a cycle of mutual distrust.

The military stands in the middle of these developments, torn between an impelling desire to return to political neutrality and an inclination for intervention in domestic politics. Since the transfer of power, some factions in the military have never been kept under government control. In May, 1964, following an antigovernment student demonstration, a progovernment airborne group exerted direct pressure on the Seoul district court to issue writs for the students' arrest. And on May 7, 1965, a group of seven Army officers, led by Colonel Chung Yeun Won, former Chief Secretary of Public Information to the SCNR, were arrested for having attempted a coup d'état.[8] They were tried by a military tribunal, and Colonel Won was sentenced to death. Their statements at the military tribunal provide good reasons to believe that the uncovered coup was influenced by almost the same factors as had been the military coup of 1961. Apart from the current political climate, promotional tensions are still acute in the Army. Furthermore, factional struggles have been gaining strength in the aftermath of military take-over, primarily because it was the result of a faction acting without the legitimate authority of the top commander.

In order to deal with these sources of cleavage, the military government initiated a system of compulsory early retirement. By the Military Personnel Law (January 20, 1962) and its Implementation Act (February 6, 1962), all military officers should retire according to maximum limits in rank service, total service, and age (Table 3). So far, this sys-

Table 3

MAXIMUM SERVICE LIMITS OF OFFICERS

	Rank Service Limit	Total Service Limit	Age Limit
		YEARS	
Second Lieutenant	3	—	—
First Lieutenant	5	—	—
Captain	7	—	—
Major	8	20	43
Lieutenant Colonel	8	24	47
Colonel	9	27	50
Brigadier General	8	31	54
Major General	7	33	56
Lieutenant General	6	—	60
General	—	—	60

SOURCE: Military Personnel Law, Art. 8, Para. 1.

tem has not functioned long enough to facilitate the flow of officers through the ranks and to hold out to new recruits the promise of an orderly career. There is a growing feeling of insecurity among officers facing discharge, and increasing appointments of retired officers to the bureaucracy and paragovernment organizations are a by-product of this device.

Political developments in the past six years in Korea have changed considerably the functions of the military and their symbolic place in society, and have opened the way to a new pattern of civilian-military relations. The forceful assumption of power by the military, and later the premeditated transfer of power to the military-dominated civilian government, divested the government of its constitutional cloak of authority. The military coup, led by a group of frustrated young officers, in turn projected the military onto the national scene as an interest group. It no longer appears as the sole representative of the highest national ideals but as a group struggling for power with other civilian political groups. As Korea goes into its militaristic period, its political future depends largely on the relationships of the military officers, whether in uniform or not, to the other civilian politicians, particularly the emerging forces of the younger generation.

ROLE OF MILITARY IN MODERNIZATION

WE HAVE examined the causes of military intervention mainly from the point of view of the internal social organization of the military, and also the changing pattern of civilian-military relations since the military coup. Now let us turn to the role of the military in the modernization of Korea. A proposition often encountered is that armies are powerful forces in the modernization process of the underdeveloped countries.[9] Is this proposition supported by the Korean experience? What are the capacities of the Korean military to supply effective political leadership for rapid economic development and social modernization? What are the consequences for modernization of the Korean military's economic and social activities? In seeking a realistic estimate of the role of the military in the modernization of the country it is necessary to examine non-military functions as they have been performed in Korean society.

When the Korean military officers came to power, whatever their actual motivation, they were deeply committed to the goal of "rapid modernization of the fatherland." To this goal they announced a revolutionary reform program reflecting popular demands; a program which was intended to eliminate unjust, corrupt practices from the government and society, as well as to rebuild the national economy on a self-sustaining basis. In particular, their program aimed at changing the civilian political system, and involved planned industrialization and agrarian reforms. They also promised greater benefits to the masses, proposing to curb the power of a few upper groups enriched through association with the government. Although the ambitious young officers displayed considerable initiative to lead a genuine social revolution, they failed to achieve its aims in the end.

Apparently the young officers had believed in 1961 that the country's problems could be solved if only the government displayed determination and a willingness to call for self-sacrifices. Viewing the spirit and the ethos of the civilian politicians as little more than uncontrolled cravings for corruption and compromise, they thought of themselves as enlightened members of a new, modern generation and as saviors of the nation facing a crisis.[10] Within a few months the junta members came to realize that government was an extremely complicated and intractable undertaking. The solutions were not quite so easy as they had assumed. Hence they began to compromise their original standards and take on some of the aspects of the politicians, whom they had held in contempt.

Since the national economy had been heavily dependent upon the United States, the central issue was to bring about rapid economic development as the basis of real independence. United States assistance to Korea since the Korean War had served primarily military purposes and consequently had had limited impact on economic development. In the deteriorating economic conditions, there were growing feelings among intellectuals that Korea could achieve economic development even without much assistance from abroad, provided the nation's internal economic and social life was reorganized, and that the record of modernization was much better when Korea acted on her own. Largely responding to these feelings, the military junta started down the road of "national democracy" accompanied by radical reform measures. This program introduced significant friction between Korea and the United States in the initial period of military rule. As soon as the military junta came to know, however, that it could not make any move without American support, its nationalistic political tone became superficial.

Military training did little to equip Korean officers with the necessary skills for running a country striving for rapid modernization. Because their professional career isolated them from the main currents of society, their understanding of national problems was likely to be defective. And the Korean military was not highly developed in terms of armament technology and general staff work, so that there was little carryover of their military skills to government administration. Therefore, the competence of military men for high political posts was open to serious question. The political deficiencies of the military government were further complicated by factionalism that developed within the junta. Conspiring officers, no longer united against a common foe, found the aftermath of a successful coup filled with conflicts between factions. As a result of power struggles, junta membership frequently shifted; and seven members, including General Do Yung Chang, Army Chief of Staff at the time of the military coup, were involved in two out of ten uncovered counter-coups during the period of military rule.[11]

As the junta members came to be attracted to power, the express aims of the revolutionary reform program began to be perverted. The Korean military regime was essentially a "caretaker government" because it promised a return to civilian rule. Nevertheless, it was reluctantly oriented to the problem of transferring power. In order to hold power continuously, the revolutionary officers, at last, allied with the blacklisted politicians, whom they had condemned as enemies of the people. Consequently, this system of alliance in a military-created political party did not make any contribution to political change other than to bring the military class into political prominence. The organization and the conservative mentality of Korea's political parties was left almost intact. Furthermore, corruption resulted from the problem of conserving power through the establishment of a mass political party under the direction of trusted military officers. Funds which were free from legal control were needed for this purpose. It was strongly hinted that the so-called four grave scandals under the military rule were connected with the creation of the Democratic-Republican Party.[12] It was also discovered that some military officers used their government office for personal enrichment.

The Korean military government showed a great deal of initiative in dealing with national economic problems, appropriating the advice of civilian experts. Yet, as measured by overall economic development, the experience of the military regime was hardly impressive. The outcome indicates that the military officers suffered from lack of experience in supplying central economic direction. They were particularly inclined toward ruinous financial policies, and their drive for rapid economic development led to overhasty industrialization programs. The first Five Year Economic Plan launched by the military government was too ambitious to achieve its targets in the important initial period, and the failure of its ill-conceived currency reform aggravated the economic life of the common people. There was also little improvement in agricultural sectors in which the military government equally concentrated its efforts for a combination of economic and political reasons.[13] Possibly the acceptance of the legitimacy of economic motivation was a consequence of military rule. In fact, economic matters acquired top priority and resulted in freedom for occupational groups to seek economic advantage. However, the military government's economic policies led to the resurgence of corruption among big businessmen.

COST OF THE ARMED FORCES

ONE of the chief impediments to real economic progress in Korea has been the inflated cost of the Armed Forces. Despite American aid, the

Armed Forces' share of the national budget since independence has averaged about 23 to 55 per cent annually (Table 4). The current defense expenditures represent 31.6 per cent of the total government budget, which is 4.2 per cent of the gross national product. In addition, sizable appropriations for the Armed Forces such as military pension and relief funds, amounting to nearly 3 per cent of the total budget, are carried on special accounts. Although the United States undertakes to provide all basic equipment for and to subsidize a large portion of maintenance costs of the military establishment, the defense budget of Korea is high when compared with that of the major countries (Table 5). And the share of defense expenditures is expected to increase considerably for years to come, because the United States has already begun gradually to cut back its defense support to Korea according to its military assistance transfer program. In view of Korea's limited financial resources and heavy developmental demands, the high military budget is an almost unbearable burden.

Military spendings have contributed little to the economic development of Korea because the annual defense budget is almost entirely devoted to the recurrent maintenance costs of the military establishment. In 1963, for example, over 80 per cent of the total defense expenditures was allotted to personnel maintenance costs, such as salaries, food, and clothing.[14] It is clear, therefore, that capital allocated to such military expenditures can have limited effects on industrialization. Moreover, Korea's high mobilization drains a considerable portion of available human resources into an unproductive military establishment. Above all else, the cross-sectional draft of young men at a rate of 2.2 per cent throughout the country not only has crippled an effective utilization of educated manpower, but also has caused a seasonal shortage of labor force in rural areas.

Of course, the military establishment performs important economic and social functions in Korean society. The Army has contributed to productive developments such as the construction of roads and villages and land reclamation projects. It has often assisted in relief and rehabilitation after major national disasters such as floods and droughts. In recent years it has been developing a program of agricultural production to help alleviate the nation's food shortage.[15] With some notable exceptions, however, the importance of these activities is more symbolic than economic.[17] The basic limitations of the Korean military to act in public

Table 4

DEFENSE EXPENDITURES, 1949–1966

Year	Defense Expenditures	Total Budget	Counterpart Fund (US Aid)	Gross National Product	Defense Expenditures		
					Total Budget	Counterpart Fund	Gross National Product
	IN MILLION WON: APPR. 274 WON = US $1				PERCENTAGES		
1949	23.95	91.11	0.22	—	26.3	1,088.6	—
1950	132.43	242.96	13.15	—	54.5	1,007.1	—
1951	329.84	617.86	—	—	53.4	—	—
1952	946.28	2,150.76	306.95	—	44.0	308.3	—
1953	3,260.54	6,068.31	795.89	41,620	53.7	409.7	7.8
1954[a]	5,991.81	14,239.16	4,470.43	74,650	42.1	134.0	8.0
1955[b]	10,637.88	28,143.94	15,053.63	152,715	37.8	70.7	7.0
1957	11,246.00	35,003.00	22,451.00	171,520	32.1	50.1	6.6
1958	12,732.00	41,097.00	24,580.00	182,010	31.0	51.8	7.0
1959	13,919.00	40,022.00	18,910.00	196,430	34.8	73.6	7.1
1960	14,707.00	41,995.00	16,763.00	243,140	35.0	87.7	6.5
1961	16,599.00	57,153.00	24,059.00	293,350	29.0	69.0	5.7
1962	20,474.00	88,393.00	28,725.00	338,600	23.2	71.3	6.0
1963	20,479.00	72,839.00	26,312.00	471,530	23.1	77.8	4.3
1964	24,926.00	75,180.00	28,020.00	666,720	33.2	89.0	3.7
1965	29,275.00	94,652.00	28,494.00	779,400	30.9	102.7	3.8
1966	38,536.00	121,973.00	30,921.00	908,780	31.6	127.2	4.2

[a]For 15 months.
[b]For 18 months.

SOURCE: Economic Planning Board, *1962 Budget*, pp. 100–101; *1966 Budget*, pp. 216–217, 224–225.

Table 5

DEFENSE EXPENDITURES OF MAJOR COUNTRIES, 1963

	Defense Expendi- tures	Total Budget	Gross National Product	Defense Exp.	
				Total Budget	Gross National Product
				PERCENTAGES	
United States (mil $)	53,429	113,751	585,149	47.0	9.1
Great Britain (mil £)	1,931	11,758	30,001	16.4	6.4
France (mil Frs)	16,109	90,651	391,800	17.8	4.1
West Germany (mil DM)	16,700	84,370	376,500	19.8	4.4
Italy (bil Lira)	799	5,595	28,186	14.3	2.8
India (mil Rupees)	4,739	26,136	—	18.1	—
Pakistan (mil Rupees)	905	4,826	—	18.8	—
Burma (mil Kyat)	487	1,520	8,115	32.0	6.0
Thailand (mil Baht)	1,609	9,210	68,000	17.5	2.4
Philippines (mil Pesos)	273	1,852	16,941	14.7	1.6
Japan (bil Yen)	217	2,895	21,482	11.5	1.0
Korea[a] (bil Won)	38.5	121.9	908.7	31.6	4.2

[a]Fiscal year 1966.

SOURCE: *U.N. Statistical Yearbook 1964*, pp. 582–646.

works result primarily from the imperatives of high combat readiness to meet enhanced national security requirements as well as mutual security commitments.

There can be no doubt that the military serves as a training ground for education in fundamental literacy, as well as for simple technical and administrative skills. Obviously, the mobilization and training of nearly two million of the population during and since the Korean War has had great social impact. The new recruits from rural areas received basic education; they learned some rudimentary technical and administrative training dealing with motor vehicle maintenance, sanitation, and simple skills; they were introduced to some aspects of modern life. Service in the Army has been of significance in the socialization toward modernity of a backward segment of the younger generation. In this connection, however, a serious problem arose in the course of postwar demobilization. Many of the war veterans were no longer satisfied with their prewar village life and flocked to cities where job opportunities were extremely limited. This influx became an important factor in pre- cipitating urban unemployment, on the one hand, and rural deteriora- tion, on the other.

CONCLUSION

THIS study leads to a single conclusion. The proposition mentioned at the outset—that armies are powerful modernizing agents in the under- developed countries—can hardly be supported by the Korean experi- ence. Countering the prevalent view that military elites have been the chief instrument of reform and change, military rule has not led to rapid modernization in Korea. Generally speaking, meager education, inter- nal cleavages, separateness from civilian society, and lack of appropri- ate political skills are factors that limit the capacity of the Korean offi- cers to provide effective political leadership for a country striving for economic development and social modernization. A major impediment to economic development in Korea, whether the regime is military or not, is the cost of a large standing army. The Korean military establish- ment is not only a heavy burden upon limited financial resources, it also restricts alternative utilization of available manpower.

NOTES

1. ROK Army Headquarters, *A History of Army Development.* Chungku Publishing Co., Taegu, Korea, 1955, vol. 1, pp. 3–5. Most of these organizations were leftist-oriented, so that they resisted the American at- tempt to create a South Korean constabulary. But many of their members entered the constabulary after it had been created. See Bang, Nak Yung, "The Military during the Liberal Party Era," *Shin-Dong-A* (a monthly magazine), May, 1966, p. 282.

2. Army Central Military Tribunal, *Award.* See *Kyunghyang Shinmun* (a Seoul daily newspaper), December 13, 1960.

3. The colonels leading the revolt were tried at a military tribunal, and all but one were pardoned. On the other hand, Lt. Colonel Jong Pil Kim was discharged on the charge of being involved in the revolt behind the scene. As leader of the eighth Academy class group, he played a pivotal role in planning the 1961 military coup and emerged as the man next to General

Park after the military seizure of power. For interesting information about the eighth Academy class group in regard to the military coup and post-coup political activities, see Kang, Sup, "The Eighth Military Academy Class," *Shin-Dong-A,* September, 1964, pp. 170–198.

4. Janowitz, Morris, *The Military in the Political Development of New Nations: An Essay in Comparative Analysis.* University of Chicago Press, Chicago, 1964, p. 71.

5. According to Samuel P. Huntington, a coup d'état in one political system may easily "trigger" a coup d'état by similar groups in other less-developed political systems. See Huntington, Samuel P., "Patterns of Violence in World Politics," in Huntington, editor, *Changing Patterns of Military Politics,* The Free Press of Glencoe, New York, 1962, pp. 44–47.

6. See Kim, Yung Soo, "Pre-organization of the Democratic-Republican Party," *Shin-Dong-A,* November, 1964, pp. 168–187.

7. General Park won by a close margin of about 150,000 votes in the national election, while his Democratic-Republican Party got 63 per cent of the Assembly seats with 34 per cent of the total valid votes.

8. See *Chosun Ilbo* (a Seoul daily newspaper), May 11, 1965.

9. For example, see Pye, Lucian W., "Armies in the Process of Political Modernization," in Johnson, John J., editor, *The Role of the Military in Underdeveloped Countries,* Princeton University Press, Princeton, N.J., 1962, pp. 69–90; Pauker, Guy J., "Southeast Asia as a Problem Area in the Next Decade," World Politics, vol. 11, no. 3, April, 1959, pp. 325–345.

10. Supreme Council of National Reconstruction, *A History of the Korean Military Revolution.* Dong-A Publishing Co., Seoul, Korea, 1963, vol. 1, pp. 190–194, *passim.*

11. *Ibid.,* pp. 374–385.

12. See Lee, Woong Hee, and Hyun Jin Kim, "Political Funds: Costs of Korean Democracy," *Shin-Dong-A,* September, 1964, pp 108–133.

13. General Park himself has admitted frankly that his military government made a mistake or failed in these economic and agricultural fields. See Park, Chung Hee, *The State, Revolution and I,* Hyangmun-Sa, Seoul, Korea, 1963, pp. 138–142.

14. Hwang, In Sung, "National Defense and Economic Development in Korea." Unpublished MPA thesis, Seoul National University, 1964, pp. 93–97.

15. Office of Veterans Administration, "Survey Report on Ex-servicemen's Role in Social and Economic Development in Korea." Unpublished paper prepared by Hai Dong Kim and Kyong Dong Kim, 1965, pp. 51–71.

16. Janowitz, Morris, *op. cit.,* p. 77.

PART THREE

Institutionalized Intervention

PART THREE

Institutionalized Intervention

LATIN AMERICA presents us with a host of situations of institutionalized military interventions where the military cannot promote political development and bring about political stability and where it cannot give up aspirations to rule. In the Central and South American republics the military has overthrown civilian regimes, stepped down voluntarily, or has been overthrown itself by a new military coup or by civilian-military coalitions. Springer shows how in a period of a few years the Argentine military intervened to promote civilian candidates, then took power itself, and how military factions contended for power. Argentina has been an extreme but not atypical example of institutionalized intervention.

Less clearly defined are those situations where the military has intervened two or three times and now is either directly in power (Burma) or on the sidelines but exerting influence (Turkey). The critical variable here is factionalism within the military. Factionalism can influence the propensity to intervene, as groups within the military feel they can protect themselves from rivals only by seizing power in their own name or placing power in a congenial civilian. We do not argue that only a faction-ridden military intervenes. In fact, in his case study Yalman shows how cohesion within the Turkish military facilitated the first post-Ataturk military intervention. But lack of unity within the military is, by definition, necessary for a series of military coups. Thus, the dominance of the UAR regime by Nasser and the Pakistani one by Ayub Khan have prevented counter-coups from originating within the Armed Forces. Once the military split in Turkey, and elements of it looked for civilian allies, the conditions existed for institutionalized intervention.

Interventions become a function of personal conflicts as well as policy disagreements. And each intervention leads to new grievances; interventions become built into the system as grievances accumulate and conflicts become cleavages. Korea may well be heading into this phase.

Military intervention has another consequence. As constitutional means for settling disputes and changing governments are abrogated, military intervention becomes the only way to change policies or alter leadership. Intervention even acquires a legitimacy. It becomes the habitual and finally, perhaps, accepted way of political change for groups within the military, for certain civilian leaders, and for large numbers of citizens who become bystanders to bloodless coups.

We present two examples of institutionalized intervention. Turkey struggles to avoid becoming enmeshed in the situation; Argentina is an advanced case, illustrating many of the themes we want to develop. For the Argentine military cannot disengage itself from the politics of rule; it brings not order but disorder to the country it means to serve; it does not build political institutions or construct itself as an effective political organization. The military does not bridge regional and social gaps in society; it seems to exacerbate them. Thus, in one of the most economically developed of the developing countries, the military brings neither political development nor modernization.

We shall have ample opportunity to assess the performance of military regimes in more economically backward areas as well. It will be incumbent on analysts of the military in developing areas to show how outcomes are the consequences of military rule per se. We have stressed the event of coups themselves in order to emphasize the conditions for the military's taking power and the effects of the coups. By analyzing specific coups, we have tried to cut into the structure of specific military forces in terms of social organization and political competition. And we have tried to assess the interaction of these forces with the political communities in which they live and which they so greatly influence.

Intervention and Extrication: The Officer Corps in the Turkish Crisis

by NUR YALMAN

THE coup d'état in May, 1960, which opened the door to a period of intense political turmoil in Turkey, has been followed by a series of momentous elections, starting in 1961. The most important was held in the fall of 1965, and brought about an orderly change of power. Together with the by-elections to the Senate in June, 1966, the 1965 election may be regarded as having finally placed political activity on fully legitimate tracks once again.

The free elections and the relatively easy change of power in Turkey have confounded the hasty theories of Middle East watchers who had seen nothing but a confused underdeveloped Middle Eastern pattern in the toils of the Turkish state. There has been a difference of opinion, in particular, concerning the motives of the Turkish military establishment in the period 1960–1965. Were the higher officers impatient for power for themselves, or was power thrust into their hands by the tactics of the opposition party, the Republican People's Party? To examine this question, I shall be concerned with three important incidents in recent Turkish politics and will attempt to assess the role of the Armed Forces at those points. I hope in this way to indicate as precisely as possible the role of the Armed Forces in the post-Menderes political life of Turkey.[1] In doing so, I hope also to suggest the internal structural reasons for the particular behavior of the officers corps.

The discussion is best focused by concentrating on three specific questions:

(1) Why did the Army intervene on May 27, 1960?

(2) Why did the original junta split on November 10, 1960?

(3) Why did the attempted coup of February 22, 1962, fail?

As background, it is important to note, first, the recruitment and training, in other words, the internal structure, of the Turkish officers corps; and second, the critical political conditions in which all Turkish intellectuals found themselves in the spring of 1960. The Turkish situation differs from others in the Middle East very significantly in both these respects.

INTERNAL STRUCTURE OF ARMED FORCES

TO THE outside observer, the Turkish military establishment may appear unnecessarily large, expensive, and somewhat of a luxury for a country which has been retired from the central arena of power politics for many decades. Within Turkey, however, the necessity for keeping up the best arms the country can muster is never seriously called to question. It is unnecessary to underline the real support of NATO and the United States alliances; as far as eminent Turkish statesmen are concerned, the external security of Turkey is now provided for in a fashion undreamed of only thirty years ago. These remarks are necessary to forestall any suggestion that the forces are kept up for internal political purposes. After all, throughout the long history of the decline of the Ottoman Empire the very existence of Turks (or Ottomans) in Anatolia and Rumelia was secured against constant attack by direct force of arms. Indeed, the entire episodic story of the modernization of Turkey begins in the eighteenth century with an attempt to render the military machine in particular into a more effective instrument.[2] In World War I, the Army snatched Turkey from the brink of annihilation, and in World War II, the presence of the large Armed Forces and skillful statesmanship kept Turkey from being overrun by Germany. These are the most vivid reasons, if any justification were really needed, for Turks to put much of their efforts into an efficient fighting force.

The Armed Forces consist of three Army Corps, an Air Force, and a Navy which constitute a fairly well-trained, though somewhat old-fashioned, and very highly disciplined body of 250,000 to 400,000 men. The men serve two years in the Army and three years in the Air Force and Navy. The size of the officers corps is perhaps best indicated by the simple fact that after the coup on May 27, 1960, about 235 generals and nearly 800 senior officers were retired without very serious repercussions in the functioning of the Armed Forces. (The dangerous operation did, however, occasion an anxious visit to Turkey from General Lauris Norstad of NATO).

The recruitment and training of the officers corps is important as a baseline to understand their interests and preoccupations. The recruitment of officers to all services is handled through a system of schools, from the secondary schools to the highest Military Academies. The main body of future officers enter military training in the secondary schools at the age of twelve. They wear military uniforms and are subject to strict military discipline and training. They are also to a large extent cut off from their homes. The level of education, though somewhat scholastic, is probably better than at the civil state schools. The education at these military schools is entirely free; but since they are boarding schools, the student must serve some years of compulsory service in the ranks even if he changes his mind and wants to leave military training. It should be added that the state civil educational system in Turkey is free from the primary schools to the universities.

The secondary schools and lycées (junior college level) train the cadets up to the age of twenty. It is only after about eight years of military training in boarding schools—where the students may see their families only during vacations for brief periods during the year—that entry is secured into the much vaunted Military Academy (*Harbiye*), formerly in Istanbul, and now at Ankara. After four years at this Academy, the students graduate with the rank of second lieutenant and join their regiments. They may return to the Academy at later periods for further training. Further schooling is provided for those younger officers who can successfully complete the rigorous entrance requirements of the Military Staff College. Those who succeed in getting over this final hurdle become staff officers and are distinguished from the rest by insignia and pay and usually occupy the key command posts in the regiments.

Two points in this brief description of the background of the officer corps need further emphasis: First, the recruitment is open to *all* irrespective of background who can fulfill the entrance requirements at every stage. In practice, much of the recruitment of the officer training schools comes from the middle-income groups in the cities, though considerable numbers are also recruited from the land, including many boys whose parents are small or middle-income farmers. The wealthier farmers tend to send their children to the civilian lycées and universities so that they will not be restricted later by compulsory service. Second, the long training and the organized hierarchy of military schools which funnels the candidate through a highly unified educational system provides a very strong esprit de corps for the officers compared to any other comparable group in Turkish society. Officers of all ranks enjoy very high prestige, and the military service remains one of the most important avenues for status improvement.

It is important to note that, though the officers are mainly recruited from the middle-income groups and often from old Army families, they are not identified with any particular sector of Turkish society. They are, however, "bureaucrats" in a rigid administration; and they would consider themselves, by virtue of their long and disciplined training, to be an elite corps of bureaucrats. Certainly, the formalistic love of red tape which the Turks through long and patient observation bitterly diagnose as "bureaucratic madness" is often evident in military offices. In this sense the closest affinity of the officers corps is with the ranks of the higher Turkish civil service. This affinity, which is almost an "alliance," is very significant.

The higher civil service does not have the long and unified training of the Armed Forces. Much of it is recruited from the faculty of Political Science (the famous *Mulkiye*) in Ankara. But this, too, is a top-level, mainly boarding, school, established in its present form about one hundred years ago. Entry is also highly competitive (apparently 2,000 apply for about 100 places every year), and the students are to some extent cut off from their families. The civil bureaucracy, recruited from this and other schools, also considers itself to be an elite corps in the Turkish state.

It is again relevant to point out that in my experience favoritism, graft, and bribery are extremely rare in the Turkish Armed Forces, and even relatively negligible breaches of discipline are hardly tolerated. To the best of my observations, the "cleanness" of "soldiers' homes" makes for intense feelings of honor and very high morale.

One point that is always made about the structure of the Ottoman state may be recalled here. Historians are on the whole agreed that the Ottoman state rested on the three pillars: (1) the Janissary Corps (military), (2) the Sultan and the higher civil service (administration), and (3) the *Ulema* (religious hierarchy).[3] It is perhaps noteworthy that, behind the modern façade, we can still detect the two pillars of the military and civilian hierarchies, though both the Sultan and to a large extent the *Ulema* have been eliminated.

POLITICAL CRISIS OF 1960

THE intense professional pride, long training, and military discipline of the vast organization precludes an easy involvement in politics. And indeed, throughout the single-party Republican period and later under the Menderes Democrats, until the Turkish political crisis really gathered momentum, the Armed Forces remained a highly privileged but obedient arm of the state. Their isolation from politics was fairly complete: not only were men in uniform not allowed to vote, but the entire organization was directed at the top by civilian ministers who sat in the cabinet.

Let us turn to the political situation in the context of which the coup of May 27, 1960, took place, which will also provide an answer to my first question: Why did the Army intervene?

The party of Menderes, the Democrats, had taken power in popular and free elections in 1950. The Republican Party of Ataturk, which had created the Republic and which had run the country for nearly twenty-five years, was voted out of power without much difficulty.[4] In the next (1954) elections, the Menderes Democrats had extended their mandate and had again received strong support (58.4 per cent of the popular vote). About this time, however, Menderes' impatience with the state of the economy led him to seek an active entrepreneurial role for the state. Withdrawals from the Central Bank increased rapidly, and the external trade deficit took an alarming turn. Inflation in the country was already turning many of those with fixed incomes, the intellectuals, civil servants, Army officers, and even the trading and industrial communities, against the Democrats. While the policy of easy money was not unattractive to the business circles, the necessary state controls which accompanied attempts to control prices, curb the black market, and control external trade, turned the commercial classes on the whole against Menderes. Some attempts were made within the Democratic Party to curb the power of the Prime Minister and to get rid of his close cohorts, but they were singularly unsuccessful.

An important aspect of the political situation was the censorship of the press and the increasing restrictions which began to be placed on the activities of the opposition parties. As state controls interfered more and more with the economy, Menderes evidently felt it necessary to curb the public outcry against his policies which was being raised by the Republicans. These attempts to stop the public expression of discontent were relatively mild at first. Controls were placed on the press, but were used sparingly; permission for public meetings of the opposition parties became more difficult to get. The police began interfering more and more with the activities of members of the opposition. As a result, many Democrats who felt disenchanted with this sinister turn of events defected from the ranks. Some of these formed the short-lived Freedom Party. Those who note the dynamism of Menderes' program must also recognize that the dynamism was made possible by inflation, which caused public discontent and, in turn, led him directly and inevitably to suppress the voice of the opposition against him.

The 1957 elections were somewhat chaotic. There were serious disturbances in various provinces, but the Army was called in to quell public disorder, and it did its job efficiently. The results of the 1957 elections were never officially announced. It is well known, however, that the combined opposition parties had actually secured a majority of the popular vote, but Menderes' Democrats succeeded in obtaining a crushing majority in Parliament by means of some hasty last-minute legislation.

The period which followed, from 1957 to 1960, was a state of civil war without actual hostilities. The country was divided into two feuding camps, and crises followed each other. There was, however, an important external factor in the situation. Menderes found that he could not pursue his inflationary policies because the United States, Great Britain, and Germany declined to underwrite his trade deficits. A period of economic stabilization was announced in August, 1958, and Menderes understood that he was now subject to criticism not only from those who had suffered from inflation, but also from those who had benefited and now objected to the deflationary policies. It seemed likely, in any case, that Menderes' Democrats would lose in the next elections, and hence the opposition redoubled their efforts.

In the spring of 1960, the tension in Turkey had reached a very high pitch. In ever more significant incidents in Usak, Kayseri, and Topkapi, where Ismet Inönü, the leader of the opposition, traveled, the Army was placed in the very difficult position of having to carry out orders against a person of the stature of Inönü, who was a former President of the Republic. The tension, the distant rumblings in the universities, the press, and the Army, frightened the Democrats and worried the cabinet.

Soon a bill was introduced in Parliament setting up a commission with special judicial, executive, and legislative powers. The commission was intended as a threat to the opposition and the press. It was duly rubber-stamped by the Democratic majority that Menderes commanded in Parliament. The opposition then walked out of Parliament.

The importance of this last act of Menderes, the creation of the ill-conceived special commission, in precipitating the Turkish crisis cannot be underestimated. The intentions of the Democratic high command are not yet clear, but the suggestion that it was about to close down the opposition Republican Party and clamp further censorship on the already crippled press cannot be dismissed. The threat was certainly intended, and the opposition certainly took it seriously. Menderes' weaknesses became very clear in the dramatic events which followed the fateful parliamentary decision.

Immediate and large-scale disturbances broke out in the Universities of Istanbul and Ankara (April 28–29, 1960). Riots and demonstrations by students became an everyday matter in the month of May. Martial law was declared and the major cities came under direct military rule. The demonstrations of the universities were finally topped by the quiet march of the military cadets of the War Academy in Ankara. This was a tense and dramatic moment, for the Armed Forces had finally and unmistakably shown their hand. The intention of all the demonstrations had been to induce Menderes to resign; and if he had, it seems to me very doubtful that the Armed Forces would have moved even at that late date. He did not, and when the Armed Forces took power, they did so with complete unity and almost universal relief.

Such was the situation external to the military establishment in the coup of May 27, and I should emphasize that it took two or three years or more of intense political turmoil and much wooing by the opposition politicians to induce the military establishment to act. And when they did, the country was deeply divided, certainly on the verge of very serious disorder, if not civil war. I do not think, therefore, that the reasons for the intervention of the Armed Forces in Turkey on May 27 can by any means be traced to the internal structure or to the personal ambitions of the officers corps. Such attempts to do so are unconvincing.[5]

SPLIT IN ORIGINAL JUNTA

A SINGULAR situation developed in the summer of 1960 after the May coup. Behind the anonymity of the "Armed Forces" a junta of thirty-eight had emerged and had sworn a solemn oath in Parliament to hold elections and return to normal parliamentary life at the "earliest opportunity." Of the two major parties, the party of Menderes (Democratic Party) was crushed and outlawed. But unlike Pakistan before Ayub Khan and unlike Egypt before Nasser, the politicians were by no means all discredited. On the contrary, the Republican opposition, which had provided the real resistance against Menderes, was greatly admired both within the military establishment and outside among the political intellectuals in the universities, the press, and the civil service.

For various reasons, the junta, which considered itself to stand for national unity—and, incidentally, continued to wear uniforms—was reluctant to join the Republican Party and publicly take sides in the civil conflict which had raged for several years. On the other hand, it was also clear that the Republican organization stood firm in the country, and provided the base for the organized expression of opinion. The junta, in contrast, had no organization linking it with a base of popular support and with which to gauge and rally public opinion. The thirty-eight members, who were of diverse ranks, were soon looked upon with some suspicion by the rest of the Armed Forces.

Even though there was no direct expression of differences between the junta and the Republican Party, it was well known that the Republicans wanted speedy elections and an end of junta rule.[6] It was precisely on this issue of the timing of elections that some members of the junta began to drag their feet. And hence an initial crack made its appearance inside the junta which became obvious to those who watched them very closely that summer.

The junta had been constituted to establish maximum communication between the conspirators and the ranks of the officers corps. There were some members from most of the ranks included in the group. However, apart from some limited number of first lieutenants, captains, and majors, and apart from five generals (two full generals, one of them, Cemal Gürsel, Commander-in-Chief of Land Forces under Menderes, and head of state until a few months before his death in 1966), the majority of the junta members were lieutenant colonels and colonels. It is noteworthy as an example of the effect of professional service that the split in the junta reflected the ranks of the officers quite directly. The two wings of opinion can be referred to as "activists" and "conservatives" and it is interesting that all the generals and almost all the colonels were on the conservative wing, whereas the younger and junior officers led again by one ambitious colonel and some lieutenant colonels were on the radical side. This point has been carefully observed in the Turkish press.[7]

Even though all members of the junta had taken oaths in the Parliament building in the summer of 1960 to return to a normal democratic order as soon as possible, whether to do this or not became an issue in the junta meetings even a few weeks later. Toward the end of the summer, it was said that junta meetings were becoming increasingly stormy and that even fist fights had occurred in closed sessions.[8]

The generals wanted to extricate themselves from the delicate and difficult situation and some at least wanted a return to their military posts. Indeed, it is said that General Madanoglu (who actually led the coup) had gone back to his office in the Logistics Department of the Army High Command the day after the successful coup and had been under the impression that, having done his "duty" to topple Menderes, he could get back to work again. The head of the junta, General Gürsel, was himself undecided as to the next steps. He certainly did want to remain in political life but realized it could not be done on the basis of a junta. The rest of the conservative wing felt that as soon as the political trials were over, elections should be held and the thorny task of running Turkey should be handed back to the politicians.

The activist wing, whether by conviction or the logical result of their desire to stay in power, claimed that they saw no future hope for Turkey under democracy. At first they merely wanted extra time—a few years —to put the country into order and then give up power, as if to postpone the evil day of democratic chaos and cynical politics. Later they began to develop some idea of running the country with an idealistic single party. Their main goals were economic: they had been much impressed by the Soviet achievements since the 1920's, had heard many rumors about China and Yugoslavia (but conveniently disregarded Eastern Europe). This pattern of rigid rule and a paternalistic guidance of the innocent Turkish peasants to an affluent future seemed to appeal to them.[9]

None of these ideas had been at all clearly formed before the coup. Indeed, it was almost pathetic to see members of the junta who suddenly found themselves in high positions, chairing meetings with professors and specialists in the old Parliament building, requesting aid and the formulation of some sort of a policy to show them the light. On one occasion a colonel of the junta, feeling that he could take the intellectuals into his confidence, requested them to draw up a "plan of action" for Turkey, which they could then put into effect.

All this time, however, the various forces which had actually toppled Menderes—the opposition parties, the press, the universities, and the civil service—remained restive and apprehensive. Turkey since Ottoman times had been governed by men whose public and private lives

had been well known and effectively scrutinized before they had ac-
ceded to power. (Gürsel was the first President to take the oath in Parliament in uniform.) The military junta, consisting of thirty-eight un-
knowns, was certainly not accorded the popular support they had hoped
for.

The political parties rightly judged the position of the activist wing as
hopeless. They could make trouble but would be unable to secure the
power they wanted. And, indeed, short of attempts to get rid of the rest
of the strongly based parties, or of setting up their own rival party organization, there was little they could do. The trap in which the activists
found themselves is obvious in their attempts to create special bodies
within the administrative structure of the state which they temporarily
controlled to serve as spearheads for "reform." The ill-fated design for
a ministry of idealism and culture, the vague conception of Culture
Hostels and other such plans are examples of their abortive machina-
tions. The bickering over the convening of a Constituent Assembly
finally exhausted the patience of the conservatives. The split was taken
care of speedily and effectively by the senior officers of the junta. Fourteen members of the activist group were arrested and then exiled as
"advisers" to Turkish missions abroad.

The incident is instructive. It shows, first, the inability of "activists"
in the junta to use their military background and high position to
fashion an effective political base for themselves. They were prevented
in their designs not only by the presence of alternative and legitimate
political organizations, but also by their professional superiors in the
junta who demanded a speedy return to a base of legitimacy. Second,
the lack of support given to the "activists" by the Armed Forces, and to
anticipate, the refusal of the military establishment to reinstate any of
the officers who were tainted by political involvements, indeed, the
ejection of officers from the ranks into politics as symbolized by their
switch from uniform to civilian clothes, again underlines strongly the
nonpolitical aspect of the professional soldiers in Turkey. (The lack of
support for these "activists" who took over the Republican Peasants'
and Nation Party has been shown by the 1965 elections when they received 2.2 per cent of the popular vote.)

FAILURE OF 1962 COUP

WHY, then, did the officers corps find it necessary to intervene at two
crucial moments (after the elections on October 15, 1961, and Febru-

ary 22, 1962) after this split in the junta? Was there a greater politiciza-
tion of the high command after the coup d'état of 1960? We should
note that the most critical posts in the hierarchy are the Commanders-
in-Chief of the Land, Air, and Naval Forces and the Chief of the General Staff. All these generals were appointed to their posts after the
coup. These top appointments, however, are constrained in detail by
the internal regulations of the Armed Forces, and the selection could
only be made from a small number of officers who had the necessary detailed qualifications.[10] General Cevdet Sunay, the Chief of the General
Staff at the time (he was elected President in 1966), indeed, was the
same person who was Deputy Chief of the General Staff for the last
years under Menderes. As a full general of the most professional type,
his main interest seems to have been the discipline and efficiency of the
Armed Forces under these trying conditions.

It should be noted that special care had been exercised not to permit
any controversial figures to return to the ranks. Not only was the rule
strictly applied to those who were members of the junta, some of whom
did want to rejoin the ranks but were refused, but even those who were
retired by the initial purge of the first junta in its enthusiastic days were
not permitted to return to the service. There is little doubt that internal
discipline was the overriding consideration in the minds of the commanders. In its internal relations, therefore, special efforts were made
to isolate the military establishment as far as possible from politics. On
the other hand, there was also a definite policy on the part of the high
command to bring the views of the Armed Forces to the parties at the
highest level and to hold the ring for the political activity of the parties
around inflamed issues. Hence meetings between the senior commanding officers and the government became a usual feature of politics in
Ankara.

Some qualifications to these remarks are called for in one respect.
During the period when the "activists" were busy in the junta, their
leader Alpaslan Türkes—then Permanent Secretary to the Prime Minister—had succeeded in placing many of his close associates in key positions in the Armed Forces and elsewhere. There was no misunderstand-
ing that control of the forces, particularly around the capital, was a
necessary part of wielding power both inside the junta and in the country at large. It would appear that one of these officers (Aydemir) was
the commander of the Military Academy in Ankara which played a
prominent role in the attempted coup of February 22, 1962. The "conservative" wing in the junta used similar tactics, and two of the influen-

tial members of this wing remained in command of large forces after the coup (Koksal, Commander of the Presidential Guard, and Madanoglu, Commander of the Ankara garrison). This was the base of strength which proved critical in the exile of the fourteen activists.

The political conditions again hold the key to the behavior of the officers. The important political events after the exile of the fourteen activists are, first, the execution of Menderes and two former ministers of his government, and second, the general elections of the fall of 1961. There is little to be said about the former except that there was no likelihood that Menderes could have been saved in the circumstances. He was a great orator and would have proved a very dangerous adversary to those who had taken a stand against him if he ever regained the public platform.

The conduct and the results of the 1961 elections are again vital to an understanding of the role of the officers corps. Soon after the exile of the fourteen (November, 1960), a Constituent Assembly was formed to deliberate and ratify the newly written Constitution, which contains elaborate safeguards against the abuse of executive power. After the Constitution was passed by the Constituent Assembly, the electorate in a referendum accepted it by a large margin. However, there were many abstentions. Finally, after this procedure of scrupulous legality, general elections were held. The results were not strikingly different from earlier elections, though they caused deep and lingering disillusionment among anti-Menderes Republican intellectuals who had hoped that, after all the turmoil and tragedies, the electorate would be less friendly to the inheritors of the Menderes mantle and would give the Republicans a clear mandate. In fact, with proportional representation (in contrast to earlier Parliaments which worked on the majority system), a complete deadlock had developed between the major parties. The Republicans had the edge in the House of Representatives, whereas the neo-Democrats (Justice Party) had the edge in the upper house. This deadlock was disastrous; for it committed the country to unstable coalition governments and once again, after all the effort, frustrated the plans of the military high command to retreat from the hotly debated political arena and leave politics to the parties. Thus, a new pattern, in which the Armed Forces pushed the parties together and forced them to cooperate and laid down the basic gentlemen's agreement to avoid specific dangerous issues (amnesty and legitimacy of the May coup), began to develop.

Here we must pause briefly: Why did the officers' corps feel that they could not leave the political arena entirely to the parties? As a simple answer, it could be said that the Army did not trust the parties other than the Republicans, even though the neo-Democrats were led by the retired General Gümüspala, Commander of the Third Army at the time of the coup, but the basis for this lack of trust is a complex matter.

In the first place, the ancient rift in Turkish public opinion between westernizing radicals and Islamic conservatives must be taken into account. I have already discussed this issue extensively elsewhere.[11] There have been modernizing reformist movements in the Ottoman Empire from the day of its first defeats at Vienna. The reformers have always had to contend with strong conservative reactions from the religious element, the court, the larger landlords, and other vested interest groups in the country. The Imperial Rescript of 1839, the constitutional movement of 1876, the Young Turks, the Declaration of the Second Constitution in 1906, and finally the creation of the Republic—to list only the incidents in recent history—are all part of this contrapuntal story of further westernization in Turkey. Since the constitutional edifice of the Republic is by now in formal terms completely "westernized," the bitter disputes have lost some of their meaning, but all controversies on the place of religion and tradition in Turkey are still fought with the ancient armory of arguments between the "Reformists" and the so-called "Backwardists."

Second, the Republicans, with their mild socialism (*étatisme*) tend to represent the interests of salaried persons, and of the middle classes. They have, therefore, the support of the bureaucrats and of the officers corps. Again, the Army since the abolition of the Janissary corps, and the civil service, is strongly identified with the "reformist" wing, to which much of the middle class may be added.[12] Menderes, who at first did have the support of this class, turned increasingly to religion to whip up support for his party among the peasantry, and finally became identified by the intellectuals with the "backwardist" wing in Turkish politics. And hence the dispute between the Republicans and the Democrats is sometimes interpreted as part of the same pattern of reform and reaction by Turkish political observers.

Third, the Armed Forces were identified with the "legitimacy" of the May 27 coup d'état, and the execution of Menderes. They therefore reacted very strongly to attempts to rehabilitate Menderes, or his party, or to throw doubt on the legitimacy of the May coup. And, in one way or another, the parties which had formed against the Republicans on the fragments of the old Democratic Party, did have to harp on these themes to gather the Menderes supporters to their ranks. It is this last issue which was uppermost in the political controversies of Turkey in 1962–1963. The other two issues, though not unimportant, were secondary.

As a result of these concerns which tended to isolate the neo-Menderes parties from the Army (and, it may be added, from the universities, civil service, intellectuals, and others who stood against Menderes), the high command of the Army was moved to impose certain limitations on the freedom of action of the political parties.

The Armed Forces intervened as a solid bloc for the first time when the new Parliament was about to convene after the 1961 elections. Dramatic meetings were held between the leaders of the political parties and the high command representing the Armed Forces: that is, the Commanders-in-Chief of the three services and the Chief of the General Staff. The junta, which had technically ceased to exist, was not represented.

The military leaders wanted explicit guarantees on the following issues:

(a) No exploitation of the question of the legitimacy of the May coup or the execution of Menderes.

(b) No exploitation of religious issues.

(c) No early amnesty of political prisoners (which would throw doubt on the legitimacy of the coup)

(d) No return of the officers retired after the May coup to the Armed Forces. (This is obviously a crucial question of unity and depoliticization in the forces.)

Only after a protocol was signed between all the parties was Parliament allowed to convene.

The situation in which the Armed Forces and political parties found themselves in 1963 was therefore simple but difficult to handle. On the one hand, the Army was identified with the legitimacy of the May 27 coup, from which it follows that the punishments meted out by the High Court (that is, the execution of Menderes) were justified. On the other hand, the parties which returned to Parliament after free elections on the Menderes legacy demanded political amnesty for the rest of the Menderes supporters, which carried the inevitable implication of the illegitimacy of the May coup.

In dealing with this problem, Inönü, then Prime Minister, went straight to the heart of the matter and said that the question of "amnesty" must be entirely separated from the "legitimacy" of the May coup. The coup was "legitimate," and the Armed Forces correct in intervening, and yet political amnesty should be accepted on humanitarian—not to speak of political—grounds to bring internal peace to Turkey.

The two parties operating under the Menderes mantle did not exercise much self-restraint on the issue of either amnesty or legitimacy, and thereby found themselves face to face with the Armed Forces. The skillful maneuvers of the government and of the leaders of all the parties were unable to stem the tide of indignation on either side. The attempts to question the May coup also caused violent reactions in the press and the students' unions, who agreed with the Army position, and this finally led to massive demonstrations against the Menderes camp. (Accounts of repeated demonstrations on April 28–29, 1962, were reported in the Turkish press.)

It was concerns such as these which had led first to the intervention of the high command at the initial opening of Parliament, and later on February 22, 1962, to an ultimatum by a group of junior officers to the government and the parties. In the ultimatum, the junior officers demanded an expulsion of about two hundred Menderes deputies from Parliament and a return, in effect, to a revolutionary Ataturk-type single-party domination. If their demands were not met, they said that they would take over and carry through their reforms. (Note that this is another version of the views of the fourteen activists, some of whom were apparently in league with the junior officers.)

Their attempt failed completely. First, the government, and in particular Inönü, refused to accept any ultimatums but the resignations of the officers concerned. Second, the military high command considered the independent action of the junior officers (led by the commander of the Military Academy) to be a breach of discipline. Third, the commanders of the Army units elsewhere in the country did not support the position of the conspirators. And fourth, the commander of the Air Force (Tansel)—who himself played an important part in all the negotiations between the high command and the parties —decided to teach these junior officers a lesson and delivered an ultimatum from a bomber squadron in midair on the grounds of discipline. So the attempted coup fizzled, but the political issues which brought it about remained unsolved and continued to exercise the officers corps as well as the other elements which were instrumental in producing the May 27 coup, up to the October, 1965, elections.

I will again underline the real desire of the professional Armed Forces in Turkey in this period to extricate themselves from politics and to return to their task of military security in a very troubled area.[13] But as long as the legitimacy of the May 27 coup remained an issue in Parliament, and as long as the amnesty of political prisoners was attached to it, the high command was directly implicated and was unable to turn away from politics.

One unfortunate aspect of all this agitation was to exacerbate the cleavage between, first, the Republican Party and the neo-Menderes camp; second, between westernized reformers and conservatives; third, between the middle classes and the sections of the peasantry which supported Menderes in the Turkish polity. At times during the crisis, the religious issue, which divided Turkish society until recently, fell into the background. The split in the Turkish polity took on more and more of the aspect of middle-class interests in some opposition to the interests of the lowest classes and the peasantry.[14] Menderes was a great orator who promised paradise to the lower classes, and threatened mainly the salaried middle classes. The Army and the Republicans, the universities and much of the press, who are identified precisely with these interests, did not look with favor on a neo-Menderes revival.

In these respects there appears to have been some parallel between the political fortunes of Argentina and Turkey, both of which, according to some observers, are economically in similar straits.[15] The crisis engendered by free elections in a polity where popular leaders may capture the imagination and votes of the lower classes, but where the bureaucracy and the middle class retains effective power and feels its interests threatened, may make an interesting study in political dilemmas.

CONCLUSIONS

WHAT conclusions may be drawn from this analysis of the role of the officers corps in Turkey?

First, the idea that the Army and the higher civil service is charged with the responsibility for the "destiny" of Turkey, as opposed to the electorate, remains important and continues to trouble the unhindered exercise of parliamentary politics. An example may be seen in the "ultimatum" of the military high command to the Parliament as recently as the fall of 1964.[16]

Second, this idea itself stems from the traditional role of these elite groups in Turkey and is very different from the background of army coups d'état in other countries in this region.

Third, the Justice Party will be able to achieve results in Parliament only when trust is reestablished between them and the elite groups. Recent developments in Turkish politics, such as the great success of the neo-Democrat Justice Party at the polls (60 per cent of the popular vote in the June, 1966, election), already show a strong movement in this direction.

NOTES

1. For an admirable analysis of the role of the officers at an earlier period, see Rustow, Dankwart A., "The Army and the Founding of the Turkish Republic," *World Politics,* vol. 11, no. 4, July, 1959, pp. 513–552.

2. The most authoritative work on this far-reaching issue is Lewis, Bernard, *The Emergence of Modern Turkey,* Oxford University Press, New York, 1961.

3. Gibb, H. A. R., and Harold Bowen, *Islamic Society and the West,* vol. 1. Oxford University Press, New York, 1950.

4. See Karpat, K., *Party Politics in Turkey 1945–56,* Princeton University Press, Princeton, N.J., 1959.

5. For example, see Lerner, D., and R. D. Robinson, "Swords and Ploughshares," *World Politics,* vol. 13, no. 1, October, 1960, pp. 19–44, which refers to the effects of American aid on the Turkish Army, followed by an account of the Highway Program of the Ministry of Public Works. The authors claim in effect that the Turkish officers moved because they were ambitious and frustrated. They emphasize that their evaluation is "a direct challenge to observers who have, in recent years, pointed out the serious deficiencies of the Republican regime in Turkey." Their argument contains no reference to inflation, hardly mentions the acute political crises and tension, and says nothing about Menderes' hectic attempts at censorship or street gangsterism.

6. See, for instance, Colonel Turkes, who claims that Inönü was full of passion for power, "like a young man on his wedding night." *Durum,* June 2, 1966, no. 86.

7. See, for instance, *Akis,* Ankara, March 5, 1962, p. 19.

8. For a detailed account of the divisions inside the junta written by an insider, see Seyhan, Dundar, in *Milliyet,* May 27, 1966.

9. See some of their ideas in *Ulku,* published in Ankara; see also the recent revelations of Colonel Turkes in *Durum, loc. cit.*

10. Compare, for example, with Indonesia: ". . . Sukarno installed a military style 'Economic Operations Staff.' . . . The governor of the National Bank became an army major general; the Chief Minister became a full general; the Foreign Affairs Minister became an air force vice marshal; the Distribution Minister became a rear admiral." *Time,* May 4, 1962.

11. "Westernized Reformers and Reactionary Conservatives: The Major Cleavage in the Turkish Polity." Unpublished manuscript.

12. For the role of Military Schools in the New Ottoman Movement, see Ramsaur, Ernest E., Jr., *The Young Turks: Prelude to the Revolution of 1908.* Princeton University Press, Princeton, N.J., 1957.

13. See "Turkey Looks Both Ways," *The Economist,* April 15, 1961. (*The Economist,* which has a brilliant Ankara correspondent, has on the whole given the best coverage to the Turkish crisis.)

14. Gunes, T., "Aydinlarin Diktatorlugu" (Dictatorship of the Enlightened), *Hur Vatan,* Istanbul, February 20, 1962.

15. Rostow, Walt W., *The Stages of Economic Growth.* Cambridge University Press, New York, 1960, p. 1.

16. See also Prime Minister Suleyman Demirel's analysis of the June, 1966, by-elections: When the Republicans and the Worker's party really begin to respect the will of the electorate, the troubles of Turkey will be over.

Disunity and Disorder: Factional Politics in the Argentine Military*

by PHILIP B. SPRINGER

BECAUSE military politics is normally closed to public scrutiny, the military is usually considered an internally undifferentiated unit acting in the political arena. An examination of the Argentine experience of recent years, however, reveals a picture of faction-ridden Armed Forces. The Argentine military is not monolithic; nor is it a caste. The notion of the Army as caste implies that the military is an autonomous stratum acting in terms of a self-generated interest. In reality, the military is linked at many points to a variety of social and political groups and is particularly responsive to its social environment.

A study of a conflict between factions of the Argentine Army in 1962 was undertaken to answer the following questions: Why did the unusual event of an armed clash within the military occur? What attitudinal differences were there between and within factions? What were the social bases of the factions? How stable were the factions over time? What consequences did the victory of one faction have for changes in the political system?

An understanding of military factions shows the complexity of what otherwise might be an oversimplified image of politics in developing nations. The military is too often regarded as having a fixed predisposition to intervene conditioned only by the resistance that civilian authority can raise. But the Argentine case shows a variety of attitudes toward military and political values of discipline and legality, which change as military experience in politics itself changes.

THE AZUL-COLORADO CLASH

IN SEPTEMBER, 1962, two factions in the Argentine Army came into open conflict. The Azules (or "Blues," a word which means "our side"

* This study is based on research conducted in Argentina from July, 1965, through June, 1966, when the author was a Research Associate of the Center for Social Organization Studies, University of Chicago.

in the terminology of war games) revolted against the high command of the Army, composed of the Secretary of War, José Cornejo Saravia; the Commander-in-Chief, Juan C. Lorio; the Chief of Staff, B. Labayru; and their allies. The Azules called these opponents the Colorados (meaning "Reds" or "the enemy"). After four days of fighting, during which several soldiers were killed, the victorious leader of the Azules, General Juan Carlos Onganía, accepted the surrender of the Colorados and removed them from positions of military command. In the midst of the conflict, José M. Guido, the President of Argentina, had gone over to the side of the Azules, and he continued in office with the support of General Onganía.

This conflict between the Azules and Colorados originated in the post-Peron period when new kinds of military-political men developed among those officers who had played important parts in the "Liberating Revolution" against Peron or who had held key posts in the postrevolutionary government of the provisional President, General Pedro Aramburu. Many of these men, who had been in retirement during the last stages of the struggle against Peron, returned to active military service after long periods of engagement in political conspiracy and were no longer prototypes of the purely professional officer. Since political activity was tolerated, factions arose in the officer corps. The bases of differentiation among these officers, such as social background, education, membership in one or another branch of the Armed Forces, tended to be converted into political groupings.

It was this situation that Arturo Frondizi confronted when he took office in mid-1958. Frondizi had come to power through the votes of Peronists, who were legally proscribed from presenting their own candidates. Once in office he found that his authority was in fact quite limited. The military leadership was constantly issuing *planteos* or demands to make Frondizi change the policies or personnel of his government. Many of these officers were allied with the People's Radical Party, which Frondizi had defeated and with which they shared a distrust of the administration's petroleum policy involving contracts with foreign companies for exploration and drilling. This policy was considered an *entrega* or sell-out to "foreign monopolies."[1]

During Frondizi's term some military officers and units attempted to defend him against his military opponents. When an anti-Frondizi general, Carlos Toranzo Montero, attempted to rename himself Commander-in-Chief of the Army after being removed, these officers offered to resist him. However, Frondizi wished to avoid violence and gave in to the rebel. His would-be defenders later became prominent in the Azul movement. A clash of factions was avoided because the President had authority over the professionalist faction that sought to defend him. At the same time Frondizi's policy of concessions kept his opponents temporarily satisfied.

Ultimately, Frondizi was overthrown. He discouraged those who wanted to defend him and failed to satisfy those who wanted to be rid of him. The occasion of his fall in March, 1962, was the election of a Peronist trade-union leader as Governor of the Province of Buenos Aires. Frondizi annulled the Peronist victory, thereby stripping himself of the legality which had been his only support. Once he himself had violated it, he could no longer expect his military opponents to respect it.

The military group that overthrew him was so politicized that its factions, which cut across services, could not come together and form a military junta to maintain their rule. Thus, Frondizi was replaced by the President of the Senate, José M. Guido, who was next in line of succession. But in April, 1962, the Army commander who overthrew Frondizi was forced out by battle-ready cavalry units. These forces were encouraged by such civilians as the Minister of the Interior, Rodolfo Martinez, Jr., and his Undersecretary, Mariano Grondona, who had been in the government and were identified with a "legalist" or antidictatorship position. Soon after, the groups who had forced out Frondizi in March rebelled and succeeded, because of the President's unwillingness to see bloodshed, in having their partisans placed in key ministries in August, 1962.[2] But Guido, a de facto President, could no longer perform the role of mediator that Frondizi, as a constitutional President, could. The conflict of factions was becoming more frequent and more conspicuous. Finally, the Azules revolted.

The Azules felt that they could negotiate no longer. Past experience had demonstrated the willingness of civil authority to cede to the threats of the more vocal *golpista* sector of the Colorados which, through the control of key posts and the communications apparatus, was able to win what was called "the war of the wireless." This time the Azules hoped to win a decisive victory and to make a permanent change in the military order.

First, the Azules wanted to reduce the power of the Navy, which was allied with the Colorados. Although the Navy was consistently against Peron, it kept out of politics. Peron usually let it alone, and consequently it was less affected by the social changes which occurred during his regime than was the Army. When Peron fell in 1955, the more uniform political orientation of the Navy enabled it to play a relatively more important role in regard to policy than could the divided Army.

The second important belief of the Azules was that the Colorados were destroying military discipline and the military hierarchy. The chief of the Azules, General Onganía, declared at the beginning of the revolt that the rebellious attitudes and lack of respect for authority shown by the Colorados had damaged the Army.

Finally, the Azules believed that the Colorados wanted to set up a military dictatorship. Their political objective was the maintenance of freedom of action for the de facto President, José Guido, who had succeeded Frondizi.

Although the Azules were in agreement in regard to restriction of the power of the Navy and to the preservation of professional standards, there were various positions concerning the political content of their movement. For example, Colonel Juan Guevara made a separate declaration of rebellion in his Memorandum of August 30, 1962. Although he agreed with all of Onganía's criticisms of the Colorados, he offered a different solution, proposing that the Azules take power in place of José Guido, whom he called a "puppet and irresponsible chief of an empty government." He maintained that "neither the civil power which undercut authority" (by not resisting political pressures from the *golpistas*) "nor the insubordinate military officers have sufficient leadership qualities to attempt the simple and great work of giving again to the Nation the real force of its laws, and to the Republic, its necessary majesty." He therefore affirmed "that facing such a state of anarchy, the men of arms that have demonstrated a spirit of order, correctness, obedience and capacity of command, are the only ones that are in condition to reestablish the fundamental norms of the Argentine community: the Constitution and the Law."[3]

An examination of the surprisingly easy defeat of the Colorados in September reveals some characteristics of that faction. The Colorados had held the country in their grip for years through their opponents' fear of bloodshed. Now they had surrendered after only the most perfunctory attempt on the field of battle to maintain power. It appears that Generals Labayru and Lorio of the Colorado High Command thought that the issues at stake did not warrant a fratricidal struggle, but that they should be resolved through political negotiation. When that failed, the game was over.

To some of the Azules, the poor showing of the Lorio-Labayru forces proved that the Colorados were bad professionals, that their overpoliticization debilitated their fighting capacity. Others believed that General Lorio actually was a capable professional, as he had taught military strategy at the War College for years. They thought that the will to win was more necessary than expertise in these skirmishes.

Some Colorados agreed with the Azules. They were disappointed with the leadership of Labayru and felt he did not really want to win. Some hinted at betrayal. They felt Labayru really wanted a return to legality and free presidential elections in which Aramburu could run and be elected. Labayru, who had been very close to Aramburu, formerly as Chief of his Military Household, was supposed to have believed so strongly in Aramburu that he could not conceive of his losing that election.

This belief in Labayru's weakness or indecision, for whatever motive, is shared by high Naval officers of the "antilegalist" school. They felt that Labayru's failure to accept offers of Naval support was disastrous. Certainly it is difficult to answer why the Colorados fought alone without the participation of friendly forces from another service.

Like the Azules, the Colorados were not unified in their opinions. The Lorio-Labayru group was chiefly concerned with avoiding the return of Peron or of Peronism to power. Another group, which included many Air Force officers and the Toranzo Montero brothers, wanted a military dictatorship brought about by revolution and emphasized anticommunism. A third group, in the Navy, was also dedicated to opposition to Peronism, but in addition envisioned a neoliberal economic policy imposed by a dictatorship. This policy, they felt, would weaken the Peronist appeal to the masses.

THE AZUL LEGALISTS

AT THE end of the conflict between the Azules and the Colorados in September, 1962, a final communiqué, Number 150 of the Campo de Mayo, was issued. It called for constitutional rule upon which internal peace, national union, and prosperity must be based. Popular sovereignty was said to be the principal guideline of constitutional life. Free elections and the subordination of the Armed Forces to civilian power were essential. The military was put forward as the guarantor of the constitutional pact.

This document was written at the request of General Onganía by Colonel Julio Aguirre and his civilian friend Mariano Grondona, the former Undersecretary of the Interior under Martinez. Aguirre was an influential "professional" staff officer and also a "legalist" who wanted a government based on popular support. He and Grondona both agreed that successful economic development required a government which the working class would accept; and, like some other Azul officers, he regarded the Colorados as agents of the cattle-and-sheep men who wanted to preserve the traditional pastoral economy of Argentina. He wanted the government to take an active role in encouraging such steps toward modernization as the great irrigation and hydroelectric complex at El Chocón.

Julio Aguirre belonged also to another group of officers, mostly of upper-class origins, who, though not in agreement with all of his political ideas, also upheld professionalism and legality, wanted to keep Guido as President, and wanted to have free elections in 1963. The leaders of this group, like Aguirre, were all opposed to the "sovietization" of the Army, a process which was allowing officers to judge their superiors and their decisions.[4] They believed that dictatorships belonged to the past and that modern Argentina needed constitutional government. They had a doctrine at a moment when a doctrine was needed to legitimate their cause before public opinion. This group of officers expressed the ideology of the Azul movement in the slogan: "We are fighting so that the people may vote. Will you fight so that they *cannot*?" This slogan was publicized throughout September and produced great popular sympathy for the Azul troops, who were cheered when they marched through the workers' district of Buenos Aires.

SOME DIFFERENCES BETWEEN THE AZULES AND THE COLORADOS

AN ANALYSIS of approximately seventy leading figures from these two factions of the Army shows that more Azules come from the upper classes than do Colorados.[5] The leading Azules are all upper-class cavalry officers, and most of these men believe that the Army is the backbone of the nation. Anything like "parallel hierarchies" which exist apart from the chain of command or like a "military parliament" is, they believe, a menace; this feeling is the basis of their antagonism toward the *golpistas,* or Colorados. They value tradition and regard the Army as its embodiment, and are deeply conscious of the important role played by the military in the history of the nation, a role more important in Argentina than in most countries. They remember the role in the national organization, the federalization of the Port of Buenos Aires, the "Conquest of the Desert" which incorporated much of the national territory, the military factories which have contributed to the development of heavy industry in the national economy, and the universal conscription which instills nationalism in the immigrant or the native outside the mainstream of Argentine society.

Because the "Army" ranks high in their scale of values, these officers, who opposed the *planteos* made against Frondizi, themselves conspired against Peron when his attempts to indoctrinate officers threatened the integrity of the Army. Many Azules strongly disliked and distrusted Frondizi as President, sharing the Colorados' view of him as a great Machiavellian. But he was not endangering the Army, while his enemies, the *golpistas,* were cheapening the institution and making it seem ludicrous by their antics.

Both factions include many serious anti-Peronists, but the Colorados and the Azules seem to have different reasons for their opposition. The typical Azul anti-Peronist initially opposed Peron because of his anti-Army policies. Some spent the four years from 1951 to 1955 in prison because of their fight against him. The Colorados, on the other hand, did not participate in the rebellion of 1951, were not in jail in 1955, and so were free to take part in the actual overthrow of Peron and to monopolize the key posts afterward. Their revolt was not based on Peron's actions against the Army, but on his social policies. As one Colorado officer said, Peron was mobilizing "the rabble." Although Peron himself never intended to form workers' militias, some of his supporters suggested this possibility, which stimulated the opposition that led to his downfall.[6]

The factor of social class also affects attitudes toward the political parties. The upper-class Azules, men who claim Spanish origin, look with disdain on the People's Radical Party, an attitude emanating from their conception of the vocation of the upper class in Argentina. At the turn of the century, the "oligarchy" was willing to modernize the economy, even though for a time they resisted the political participation of the middle class. Their opponents, the Radicals, had modern, democratic ideas in regard to political development, but were unimaginative in regard to the economy. In Argentina, these two aspects of modernization are not yet related. The old ideas have persisted, and explain the anti-Radical sentiment of many Azules, who claim that "the upper class made the country," and who set themselves apart from the men of the People's Radical Party, who are *chacareros* (small farmers) and small shopkeepers, descended from Italian immigrants.

Although Frondizi came from the Radicals, his men had split off from the party to form the Intransigent Radicals, and, therefore, he was regarded with more favor by the Azules. Unlike the men of the other sector of Radicalism, he was interested in industrial development, and appealed to bourgeois industrialists, many of whom were in his cabinet. This situation evoked a favorable response from the Azules, and opposition from the Colorados.

Another striking difference between the two factions is that 56 per cent of the Colorados were born in the city of Buenos Aires, while 27 per cent of the Azules were born there. Fifty-three per cent of the Azules were born in the country's interior provinces, compared to 24 per cent of the Colorados. Twenty per cent of each faction were born in Buenos Aires province.

The fact that the Azules are predominantly men of the Interior, and the Colorados, men of the Port, helps to explain the views they have of themselves and of one another. It also explains the affinity of the Colorados for the Navy, their support of foreign trade, and their openness to foreign influences. They regard the Azules, those cavalrymen from the Interior, as Nationalists, as the Azules regard themselves. Many Colorados go further and think of the Azules as authoritarians with pro-Spanish or Nazi leanings. Many, indeed, are pro-Franco. The Azules think of the Colorados as "cosmopolitans," especially open to British influence. In regard to religion, the Colorados think of themselves as more tolerant than the Azules, whom they consider archclerical.

The opposition of the Port to the Interior has had a long history in Argentina, and has been prominent in the thought of Peron and Frondizi, both of whom are supporters of the Interior. Frondizi's support among businessmen has come more from the General Economic Federation than from the Industrial Union. The former represents businessmen predominantly from the provinces, the latter from the capital. Although most of the Azules are not in favor of Frondizi, many do believe in his idea that the interests of the Port, of the exporters of agricultural products and of the importers of petroleum and finished products, are opposed to the interests of the nation.

THE CONSEQUENCES OF THE AZUL VICTORY: LEGALISM AND THE ELECTORAL FRONT

AFTER the Azul victory of September 22, 1962, many Colorado officers were retired and major changes were made in the cabinet. Rodolfo Martinez, Jr., and Mariano Grondona were again the Minister and the Undersecretary of the Interior. Professor José Miguens became adviser to the Minister. Lt. General (retired) Benjamin Rattenbach, who had been a prominent spokesman for the Azul position prior to September, was named Secretary of War. Rattenbach was considered the last remaining officer in the "Prussian tradition," both because of his German name and his belief in extreme subservience of the military to authority. Colonel Manuel Laprida was named adviser to the Secretary of War and legalist Colonel Julio Aguirre[7] became adviser simultaneously to the Commander-in-Chief and to the Secretary of War. A new and daring approach was to be made to the most difficult problem of Argentine politics: what to do about Peronism.

Many legal restrictions of political activity by Peronists remained in effect. The return of Peron was precluded. Many political leaders began to think about forming a National Popular Front which would be acceptable to Peronists, Christian Democrats, Frondizi's Intransigent Radicals, and others. The candidate for President would not be a Peronist, and the spirit of the movement was to be modern, in opposition to that of the People's Radical Party, the allies of the defeated Colorados, who were considered representative of Argentina before 1930.

The most important person supporting the Front in October, 1962, was Martinez, the Minister of the Interior. Though he had the responsibility for developing a plan for the conduct of the presidential elections, he was also occupied with the formation of the Front. He wanted General Onganía to be the candidate of the Front, since he believed that the combination of military and civil power in one person would remove a source of political instability in Argentina. Martinez persuaded the colonels close to Onganía that he must become the candidate of the Front that was being formed. The General was popular, and Martinez could use his power to "expedite" his candidacy, to which, it was believed, neither Peron nor Frondizi would be opposed. In the next few months, efforts were made, encouraged by Martinez and supported by Secretary of War Rattenbach, to unify the forces of the proposed Front and to secure its acceptance as a participant in the election.

At the same time, a sector of the Azul officers was working against these plans. Although the staunchly anti-Peronist Azules knew that the candidate of the Front would not be a Peronist in this election, he would have Peronist support, and they were worried about the next election. There were limits to their "legalism" where Peronism was concerned. There was also opposition in the Navy, most of whose officers were still on active service, even though they were in sympathy with the Colorados, because they had not been engaged in the actual fighting in September. Through the Secretary of the Navy, they tried to resist the decision of the Election Board which gave legal status to the Justicialist party, the name under which the Peronists would participate in the election.

Another source of opposition to the Front was the civilian sector. Remembering the Peron years, many upper-class civilians, especially of the older generation, communicated their anxieties about the electoral process to their friends in the officer corps. They were particularly disturbed by provocative statements made by the Peronist labor leader, Andrés Framini. Framini proclaimed, "We will not renounce our principles of a revolutionary movement that assume the total change of the structure of the country." Though Framini was not in charge of the local Peronist movement nor of negotiations within the Front, nor with the government, his outbursts were considered significant expressions of unrestrained Peronism which had learned nothing and forgotten nothing.

During the winter of 1962–1963, with Frondizi under house arrest, a split developed within his party, the Intransigent Radicals. Oscar Alende, party chairman and former Governor of the Province of Buenos Aires, was opposed to Martinez' attempts to engineer an accord between the government and the Front by means of a military candidate, General Juan Carlos Onganía. Alende wanted a free, open election in which all parties could present their candidates. He opposed efforts by men close to Frondizi who advocated that the party renounce its electoral ambitions and make a sacrifice so that a National and Popular Front could be formed. Alende was thus opposed to the renegotiations of the Peron-Frondizi pact of 1958, especially if it were again the handiwork of Rogelio Frigerio, Frondizi's closest associate. Alende expressed great disagreement with the economic ideas of Frigerio, which he considered to favor free enterprise excessively.

Onganía was aware of this concern that the Front was being limited to Peron and Frondizi and some minor parties. He moved to encourage Martinez to try to form a broader Front which would include the People's Radicals. But this was an impossible task. The People's Radicals were long-standing political enemies of Frondizi and Peron but, more important, wanted to present their own candidates for office. They had been waiting more than thirty years for the presidency and they hoped to garner all anti-Front votes.

Martinez resigned as Minister of the Interior on March 29, 1963. The first phase of the history of the Front, which was characterized by government instigation, was over. The Front was not finished, but was, without doubt, greatly weakened.

Several days later there was a revolt of most of the chief officers of the Navy in active service, along with some small groups of the Army and Navy. This was to be the last stand of the Colorados in their final attempt to regain the power lost in September.

OPPOSITION TO LEGALISM FROM
WITHIN THE AZUL COMMAND

AFTER the defeat of the Colorados on April 5, the Commander-in-Chief issued a communiqué, Number 200, which differed markedly from Number 150 of September, 1962. Number 200 attacked all aspects of Peronism. In concrete terms, it opposed the return of the Peronist regime, which it defined as: "the structure established and the systematic plan followed by the deposed dictator and his henchmen to deform the traditional style of life of our people, manifested by moral and intellectual corruption, the discrediting and dissolution of the civic institutions of the country, the elimination of adversaries by means of extortion and physical violence and the curtailing of fundamental institutional liberties."[8]

Professor José Miguens, who had written a draft of Communiqué 200, was surprised to see a completely different document disseminated. The new one reflected, as did the Navy revolt which the Azules had just suppressed, a growing preoccupation with Frontist ideas which implied Peronist participation in the forthcoming elections in some unknown way.

The new military position was now made known to the public by General Enrique Rauch, the new Minister of the Interior. Rauch, a general in active service, had been at the crest of the Azul wave in April, 1962, when he forced the resignation of General Poggi, who had overthrown Frondizi. On April 11, 1963, the day after his swearing-in, Rauch issued decrees prohibiting Peronist propaganda and political contacts with Peron. But, at the same time, he proceeded to meet alone with Peronist leaders and his undersecretary, Dr. Guillermo O'Donnell, met with Basilio Serrano, coordinator of the Front parties. O'Donnell, in the name of Rauch, suggested that the Armed Forces name a military candidate whom the parties comprising the Front (Intransigent Radicals, Christian Democrats, Peronists, and Popular Conservatives) would then accept as an "act of faith." The implication, Serrano believed, was that the candidate would be Rauch himself. Serrano and other Front figures were bewildered by Rauch's separate meetings with Peronists. The Minister's purposes were not clear to anyone. Within a short time, however, the cloud of confusion lifted.

Soon General Rauch issued a sensational memorandum in which he observed that numerous interests close to Frondizi were trying to convert legalism into an empty formula and that the election was becoming an end in itself. He proposed a minimal program of sanctions against economic crimes and corruption, and the suppression of smuggling. He continued with an attack on the honesty and integrity of a fellow cabinet member. All of Rauch's behavior led the public to feel that he was moving toward a coup d'état. Consequently, all other cabinet members, led by Secretary of War Rattenbach, resigned and put the decision of how to deal with Rauch to the Azul chiefs. Onganía presided over a meeting in which some officers advocated removing Guido and taking charge of the country, as Rauch had suggested. But one legalist officer with an important command stated that he had twice, in September and April, fought and had been prepared to die and had asked his troops to do so to defend the Constitution and free elections, and that he was prepared to do so again. With this threat of a split in the Azul forces, Onganía decided that Rauch would have to resign. He did so on May 12, 1963.

Two-and-a-half years later Rauch gave some explanation of his behavior, which had complicated understanding of the Azul movement. In an open letter to General Onganía, Rauch explained:

> ... Together with our comrades we fought against those who wanted to break the institutional order of the Nation; you in the simple and plain defense of subordination to civil power and in the sustaining of legality; I only in the sustaining of legality, as a need of the moment and to create the best conditions for the government that might come forth, as the ultimate alternative to the reigning system. ...[9]

Thus, Rauch revealed that doctrinaire legalism was not the only motive at work in the Azul rebellion. It was but a position of the moment—a counter to *golpismo*. Subordination to civil authority meant even less to Rauch. In late 1964 and throughout 1965 as a rebel and technically as a fugitive from justice, General Rauch continued to advocate the "national revolution" as Colonel Guevara advocated the "New Force," a corporatist movement he formed in 1963.

LIMITED LEGALISM: ELECTIONS
BUT WITHOUT THE FRONT

ON MAY 12, a new Minister of the Interior was designated. He was General Osiris Villegas, also on active duty. Villegas was the last Minister of Interior in the period leading up to the presidential elections of July 7, 1963. His ministry was characterized by constant harassment of Peronist and Frontist forces.

The platform of the National and Popular Front, advocating agreements with the International Monetary Fund and government collaboration with private foreign companies to assure national self-sufficiency in regard to petroleum, was approved by Frondizi and by the Peronist unions. This approval indicates that among the leaders, at least, of two important sectors of Argentine society, there is no ideological cleavage; and it also shows that the Peronist unions are not revolutionary but are willing to accept a quite conservative program.

Finding a candidate who would be acceptable to the military was the most serious problem of the Front.[10] Finally, Vicente Solano Lima was chosen in June, 1963, as the candidate for the presidency with the approval of Peron, Frondizi, and of the leaders of the Peronist unions. This minor figure from the Popular Conservative Party was chosen because the Front could not name anyone too closely identified with Peron and because Peron would not support an important man whose election might lead to his own eclipse. The military and the rank-and-file members of the union were not sympathetic to this choice.

The Front at that time would willingly have nominated Onganía as its candidate. In fact, Rodolfo Tecera del Franco, a spokesman of the Peronists, personally offered the support of the movement to the General in a private meeting, but Onganía would not run. There is still some mystery surrounding his reasons for not running for President with great support offered to him and with the opportunity for a constitutional mandate. Perhaps the best explanation is that the Azul movement was based upon a belief in civilian government. "The Army in the barracks" was the belief of the moment. Since the Azules had not revolted in order to place Onganía in Government House, it would have been difficult for him to push his own candidacy, even had he wanted to, without violating Azul convictions and commitments. Other officers in fact discouraged him by pointing to Azul norms even though not all those who were invoking them believed in them.

Thus, Solano Lima became the candidate of an unenthusiastic National and Popular Front. Four days before the election, the electors who were to cast Frontist votes in the electoral college were proscribed by the Minister of Interior, General Villegas, acting for the Armed Forces. This action was immediately followed by an abstention of the Front and the election on July 7, 1963, of Arturo Illia as President of the Republic with 24 per cent of the popular vote. His party, the People's Radicals, the civilian allies of the Colorados, came to power with Illia. The People's Radicals, who were thought to be defeated in the battles of September and April, had, through the "failure of political nerve" of the Azules, won power through elections. The Azul movement, in spite of the willingness of some of its members, failed to live up to the expectations created by Azul Communiqué 150.

The forces within the Azul movement which were dominant at the time of the election represented a limited legality: a system which was constitutionalist but which would not permit Peronist participation through a Front. "Legalism in favor of a Front" was replaced by "Legalism in favor of proscription of Peronists." This happened because the original legalist position represented the ideas of only an articulate minority of military officers and their civilian associates. As the Azules became involved with the electoral process, other, traditionalist, positions emerged among those who had been important militarily, but not politically, in September.

THE PEOPLE'S RADICALS IN POWER

WITH the coming to power of Arturo Illia on October 12, 1963, an era of party government began. The new government placed in key posts men representing different factions of the party, men who had waited years for this victory. With the men of the party came the program of the party. Petroleum contracts with foreign companies made by the government of Frondizi were annulled, and relations with the International Monetary Fund were broken off. These acts reinforced the hostility of the Azul officers to the Radicals. There were no *planteos* now, but a process of evaluation began within the officer corps of the role of the Azules in the election of Illia.

A strong force to maintain the separation of the military from politics was removed when General Onganía resigned on November 22, 1965, because of a dispute over the appointment of Secretary of War.

At this time strikes and work stoppages were becoming increasingly frequent. Government attempts to fix wage ceilings were not heeded by unions, since they had not participated in making these economic policies. This attitude was one result of the proscription of the major political force of the country in the presidential elections. The government, starting with little support, did not have much room to maneuver. It could not risk losing the little it had by making necessary but unpopular decisions. It could not govern.

The Peronist leaders, feeling no loyalty to the restricted democracy, increased contacts with military leaders with the aim of overthrowing the government of Arturo Illia. They believed that direct negotiations with the military, without intermediaries such as political parties, would benefit them more and with Illia overthrown, the military could not avoid dealing with the Peronist union leadership as it would be the most cohesive force remaining. Officers such as General Osiris Villegas, Commander of the Fifth Army Corps, and General Julio Alsogaray, Commander of the First Army Corps, were meeting with union leaders.

The new military-union dialogue was soon given publicity in mid-

March, 1966. High military officers as well as numerous Peronist leaders attended a dinner by the Light and Power Union in honor of Colonel Jorge Leal, leader of a military expedition to Antarctica. Representing the Commander-in-Chief was General Alejandro Lanusse, perhaps the most anti-Peronist of all officers. Lanusse had spent four years in Peronist jails. His meeting with militant Peronists signaled a new phase in military-Peronist relations. The Army and the unions, though separated by many great differences, both felt the need to prepare for the possibility of a post-Illia system. The military wanted support so it could govern, while the unions wanted to benefit from the future system.

Responding to the mood of preoccupation in the Army, on April 1, 1966, the Secretary of War, General Castro Sanchez, issued a memorandum written jointly by himself and his Undersecretary, General Manuel Laprida, key legalist and supporter of the Front during Guido's interregnum. This document can be considered an expression of legalist sentiment within the Army, intended to buttress the government. It states, among other concepts, that "the army . . . makes known to public opinion . . . that it does not believe in 'military government' as a solution for Argentine problems . . . that experience has demonstrated that the Army, in the function of government, is converted into a deliberative body and discipline is corrupted, which leads to anarchy destroying what so much vigilance and sacrifice have cost the institution." The concluding paragraph contains a list of the nation's problems which were of concern to the military: "the economic problems, the strikes, and . . . the uncertainty of the electoral future" were especially emphasized.[11]

This document was both an attempt to reform the government by revealing Army concerns and an attempt to pacify the military chiefs by invoking orthodox Azul ideology. The expression of military worries represents a consensus of all military officers at that time. The difference between Laprida and the officers to whom the memorandum was directed was in methods of dealing with these problems of national concern. Laprida ruled out a solution through a *golpe de estado*.

The following month an election for Governor was held in the Province of Mendoza. The Peronist forces were divided between a candidate backed by the local trade unions and the candidate supported by Isabel Peron, the wife and emissary of the former President. The government had permitted her entry into the country in October, 1965, and had allowed her freedom of movement as a tactic to weaken trade-union leaders who were in rebellion against Peron's personal rule. In this way the opposition of Peronists would be considerably weakened, or so the People's Radicals hoped. This was part of the strategy known as the "option"—"either the Peronists or us." Frondizi had tried to "integrate" the Peronists into his movement but their support for him was temporary and conditional. His strategy failed. The "option" was Illia's attempt to deal with the phenomenon of Peronism by trying to rally all non-Peronist forces, a majority of the country, around his party.

In the election in Mendoza, the Peronists lost; but they gained a greater combined vote than they had received in earlier elections. But significantly, Peron's candidate received a great victory over the man who was supported by the trade unions and local organizations and by Augusto Vandor, the most powerful union chief in the country. This "victory" of the old-style Peronism heightened military concern about the possibility of holding free elections in important provinces. It reinforced the preoccupations of the staunch anti-Peronist officers about the "uncertainty of the electoral future" which had been mentioned in the April memorandum of the Secretary of War. The election focused attention on government policies, on political strategies and economic failures, that brought about the resurgence of "returnist" Peronism.

Shortly after the Mendoza election, the "option" was put to a clear test. In a minor province, Catamarca, where the national government's party is generally expected to win, the Peronists, united this time, won a decisive victory. The "option" polarized the electors between the Peronists and the People's Radicals—90.6 per cent opted for one of these two forces. But the Peronists absorbed their allies (for example, Frondizi's Movement for Integration and Development), while the Radicals failed to gain the support of those Conservatives who in the past had given adherence. Electoral uncertainty was increasing.

On May 29, the Commander-in-Chief, Lt. General Pascual Pistarini (who had replaced Onganía in November, 1965), gave an important speech during Army Week celebrations. His words can be considered a reply to the declaration of April 1 of the Secretary of War. His critique of the "formalistic" conception of liberty was an answer to the legalism of Castro Sanchez and Laprida and to Illia's presidential message of May 1, 1966, in which the President claimed that there had been not one day of a state of siege since he took office and that there was great liberty in Argentina. To this statement the Commander-in-Chief responded:

> Liberty does not exist when men are not offered the minimum possibilities to achieve their fundamental destiny, perhaps because of inefficiency that does not provide the necessary means and opportunities, perhaps because the absence of authority has opened the way to insecurity, fear, and disintegration. Liberty also is the ambient of truth and responsibility, because the free man has the privilege of faith and of hope. Therefore liberty is injured when, for the sake of convenience, decisions are postponed, encouraging the persistence of totalitarian myths, mocking the faith of some, provoking the uncertainty of others, and originating sterile confrontations, useless spilling of blood, the discrediting of institutions that generate equally the discouragement and frustration of all.[12]

Several days later the head of the National War College, a school responsible to the Ministry of Defense, was removed from his post for allowing antigovernment literature to be disseminated. The old style of civilian-military relations was beginning to reappear. This incident was reported to have deeply disturbed Onganía, since it signaled the destruction of what he had achieved in a three-year period.

It was reported by General Villegas in mid-June that the government had offered to make changes in cabinet officers, but the Armed Forces and General Onganía had made their decision. On June 28, 1966, the Armed Forces overthrew the administration of Arturo Illia. A junta of the commanders of the three services was established and transferred the powers of government to General Onganía, who became President.

THE COUP AS COMPROMISE

THE coup of June 28 represented a point of coincidence among major factions within the Army. The anti-Peronist "traditionalists," who were an important element in the Azul coalition, had never noticeably shown a "legalist" conviction. They had rebelled against Peron, and many felt during the Guido period that the Azules should have removed Guido and directly assumed the powers of government without calling for elections so soon. Public indications of this attitude were the positions of Colonel Guevara in 1962 and General Rauch in 1963 who were strongly anti-Colorado but not Azules of the legalist breed. This faction had for a long time wanted the coup.

The "Frontists" within the Army also supported the coup. This group was willing to accept free elections in which the Peronists might win. These officers had been favorably impressed by neo-Peronist administrations in some of the minor provinces and believed that the Peronist masses should be integrated into the political system. This group included Brigadier General Juan Enrique Guglialmelli. Guglialmelli and his associates are not hard-core, doctrinaire legalists, nor are they fundamental believers in military government as the solution to the country's ills, as many of the "traditionalists" are. What is important to Guglialmelli's group is that the interest of the nation as a whole, rather than that of limited sectors, be represented in the government.[13]

The coup of June 28 was supported by the Military "Frontists" because they knew that it would be impossible to have free elections for governor in the Province of Buenos Aires in 1967. It would disturb an important sector of the country and the Army and lead to great internal conflict in the Armed Forces. They also knew a coup would follow the almost inevitable Peronist victory. This coup would alienate labor from the military regime since labor would consider, and rightly so, that the coup had been directed against them. For all these reasons the Frontists accepted the present coup as opening the way to a new national encounter.

The traditionalist and Frontist forces in the Army found support among the followers of Peron and of Frondizi. This support is reflected in the revolutionary "Message to the Argentine People," proclaimed by the junta. Announcing their desire to incorporate "the modern elements of culture, science and technology," they called for unity of the nation, saying, "it is necessary to end the policy of division and confrontation that made the possibility of joint effort illusory."

Of course, many officers lack the ideological wrappings for intervention in the political arena. They simply feel that for the military regime to survive they should reach an understanding with the "factors of power," labor as well as business. They want to do this without dealing with the politicians who, they feel, are divorced from the "real country." Negotiations which began long before the coup will continue. It remains to be seen how these interactions will be institutionalized, but it is clear in any case that the era of fanatical anti-Peronism, when there was very little contact between military and Peronist leaders, is over.

The doctrinaire legalists, who had been dominant in the ministries after the Azul victory of September, 1962, no longer had any force. The group split. Manuel Laprida opposed the coup and to the end maintained legalist orthodoxy, giving sustenance to the government in his capacity as Undersecretary of War. Laprida believed in waiting for the legal end of Illia's term of office and then allowing the formation of a broadly based coalition to elect General Onganía as constitutional President. To this belief there was first the objection that three more years of Illia would be unendurable. Second, the electoral Front had been tried once in 1963, and could not be constructed then even with the support of the government given by Martinez. In 1969, when the next elections were to be held, as many former Frontists realized, it would be even more difficult to build this coalition without support from the government. During a lengthy election campaign it would also be a difficult feat to engineer Peronist mass support for the candidacy of Onganía. The rank-and-file would need more than the approval of their labor leaders to be persuaded to vote for General Onganía.

With a coup, these problems do not exist. The Peronist leaders could support the military revolt even if it were only a "leap in the dark," as one Peronist leader stated. The staunch anti-Peronists within the military leadership are willing to accept deals with the Peronists as long as the military is the senior partner. An election would create a risk, they believe, of greater uncontrolled Peronist expansion. These arguments against the Laprida position influenced some former staunch legalists to support the coup.

Legalism in 1963 was an abstraction, empty of content and with unknown consequences. It had a great appeal then. But in mid-1966 it meant Arturo Illia and government by the People's Radicals.

With the demise of orthodox legalism the coup became the outcome of a transaction between two remaining powerful forces within the Army: the traditionalists, who were anti-Peronists and pro-coup, and the Frontists, who were open toward Peronism and not fundamentally in favor of a coup. Given these elements, the ultimate solution, a coup that was not anti-Peronist, can be understood.

Another group—perhaps the largest one in numbers—is composed of officers with less interest in politics than the others. These officers feel a strong identification with Onganía as *caudillo,* and respect him as the officer who reestablished a disciplined, professional Army. Onganía's decision to participate in the coup assured their support for the movement of June 28 and the action of the Army *en bloc.*

The recent seizure of power by the Argentine military represents a reencounter of groups which had been alienated from each other since the fall of Peron in September, 1955. This coming together of the military and of labor is an initial source of political stability. Labor leaders do not want to change the system but rather to participate in it. They do not share the fears that the Left and the deposed Radicals felt about the International Monetary Fund and about foreign investors. Tensions, however, will develop if the railroad deficit is reduced through massive firings of workers without creating new jobs for them. This is a likely trouble spot since inflation caused by swollen state bureaucracies is a major concern of the military. As one general stated, "The railroad *deficit* is greater than the *budget* of the Armed Forces."

Another potential threat to the stability of the new government is the division among the generals. Onganía has great prestige, but will he be able to restrict generals with strong personal ambitions of their own?

Possible strains between the President and the generals will be mitigated by the Azul emphasis on professionalism. The Azul Revolution of June 28 is consistent with this emphasis on professional values, since the Army acted through its institutional leader, the Commander-in-Chief, and maintained its hierarchy and discipline intact. Onganía, a retired officer, was given the Presidency. No officer in active service is a member of the government. But it remains to be seen how long the generals remain separate from affairs of state.

One problem which plagued Frondizi is unlikely to trouble the new regime. Many industrialists supported Frondizi's economic development policies but could not sympathize with his attempts to integrate Peronists into the political system or with his mildly independent foreign policy, as in the case of Cuba. Thus, they were neutral at the time of his overthrow. The military regime will be less likely to suffer defections because of an "integrationist" policy since military participation in the new system lends an aura of respectability to the regime which Frondizi never had. In the new social compact there is a minimum risk of unpleasant outcomes, such as a Peronist electoral victory.

CONCLUSIONS

AFTER the fall of Peron, a new class of military politicians arose in the Army. Many of them had been engaged in conspiratorial activity while in retirement during Peron's rule. These men and their civilian allies worked to displace the elected government of Arturo Frondizi. After years of turmoil, a new group, which emphasized professionalism, emerged in the Army and dislodged the politicized faction. This group then tried to deal with the still powerful forces of Peronism, a phenomenon which had stimulated the rise of earlier political factions in the Army. Since to many Argentinians Peronism represented a militant working class, still marching under the banner of a dictator, it threatened to cause violence if it were allowed to play a part in the electoral system, and violence if it were excluded from it. Various solutions had been attempted: suppression, by Aramburu; integration, by Frondizi; the Front, by Martinez; the option, by Illia. None worked. The Azul revolution of June 28, 1966, was an attempt to solve the problem of political disunity in Argentina.

There will probably be attempts to establish authoritarian government which holds out some hope of maintaining social peace while permitting further economic development. However, the history of recent Argentine politics shows that the military acting without popular support cannot stabilize the country. At the same time, a government without military support is equally unstable. The regime of Peron lasted for more than a decade because it combined Army support and popular support for a leader who mediated both sectors and did not fully surrender himself to either.

The military ultimately cannot avoid the challenge of political intervention in a society faced with crises in economic and social development. Different factions have varying styles and propensities for intervention. Intervention by one faction is a response not only to social problems but also to previous interventions by other factions. Thus, military intervention in political life has become institutionalized in Argentina.

NOTES

1. Compare this attitude with an observation made about the Radicals of fifty years ago. "The silence of the Radical Civic Union in regard to key

problems of the economic process and its reaction of 'moral indignation' in the face of the emphasis that its opponents put on economic activity represent, to a certain degree, a recourse to values of a traditional type." Gallo, Ezequiel, Jr., and Silvia Sigal, "La Formaçion de los Partidos Politicos Contemporaneos: La Union Civica Radical (1890–1916)," in di Tella, T., and others, editors, *Argentina, Sociedad de Masas,* Editorial Universitaria, Buenos Aires, 1965, pp. 128–129.

2. During the Frondizi period, officers who were constantly pressing Frondizi became known as *golpistas*. By and large, these were the same men who became known as Colorados.

3. *La Razón,* August 31, 1962. Guevara's statement shows how an officer could be professionalist and against the *golpista* style of the Colorados and, at the same time, willing to advocate a military dictatorship. In Guevara's thinking, professionalism does not inevitably lead to a belief in civilian rule. But at that time, Guevara was marginal to the military-political groups dominant within the Azul movement.

4. Along with Aguirre, Colonel Roberto Arredondo, Colonel Lopez Aufranc, and Colonel Manuel Laprida were in this group. Their ideas were nurtured when they were all in Europe together at the same time in the late 1950's. Aguirre was military attaché in London; Laprida in Brussels; Arredondo was with the Argentine military attaché's office in Paris; and Lopez Aufranc was studying in Paris. Three of the four were sons of military officers; all but Aguirre remained in active service during Peron's regime. The hard-core Azul legalists are tied together through class background, membership in exclusive clubs, or through past attendance at elite *colegios* where the military men have come into contact with civilians of legalist persuasion who were to play an important advisory role within the Azul movement. Besides Martinez and Grondona, we refer to Professor José Miguens, author of most of the Azul communiqués and adviser on psychological warfare.

5. See de Imaz, José Luis, *Los Que Mandan* (Eudeba, Buenos Aires, 1964, pp. 58–61) for data on the middle-class origins of generals. Such aggregate data do not show the upper-class origins of the Azul movement. Therefore, data on individuals were obtained from military biographies, received from the Argentine Secretariat of War.

6. Interviews and speeches also reveal a clear difference between Azul and Colorado attitudes in respect to Peronism vis-à-vis communism. The Azules, even though many were hostile toward Peronism, consider it a national force and a bulwark against communism. The Colorados consider it a stepping stone on the road to communism. These attitudes have affected the relations of the military factions with the Peronist movement.

7. Aguirre is the representative military-political figure of the period following the Azul victory. He symbolized the juncture of concerns for legality and free elections.

8. *La Razón,* April 6, 1963.

9. *Ibid.,* December 2, 1965.

10. The military chiefs, especially General Onganía, were not helpful in making suggestions. The colonels in the War Ministry, though weakened after the fall of Rodolfo Martinez as Interior Minister, were still frequently meeting with Frontist politicians. The colonels would suggest what politicians might be acceptable to the military, but these initiatives had little backing from the high command.

11. *La Razón,* April 2, 1966.

12. *Ibid.,* May 30, 1966.

13. Guglialmelli was a "legalist" in 1963, opposed to the prescription of the National and Popular Front, because he wanted a broadly based movement to come to power. In 1966 he was no longer a "legalist" since he now felt that only through a coup could this be achieved.

INDEX

Index